DUBLIN 1916

DUBLIN 1916
THE SIEGE OF THE GPO

CLAIR WILLS

Harvard University Press
Cambridge, Massachussetts
2009

© 2009 by Clair Wills
First published in the United Kingdom in 2009 by
Profile Books Ltd
58 Hatton Garden
London EC IN 8LX

Printed and bound in the United States of America

Library of Congress Cataloging-in-Publication Data
Wills, Clair.
Dublin 1916 : the siege of the GPO / Clair Wills.
p.   cm.
Includes index.
First published in the United Kingdom in 2009 by Profile Books, London.
ISBN 978-0-674-03633-8 (alk. paper)
1. Ireland—History—Easter Rising, 1916.   2. General Post Office (Dublin,
Ireland)—History.   I. Title.
DA962.W64 2009
941.7082′1—dc22
2009008440

CONTENTS

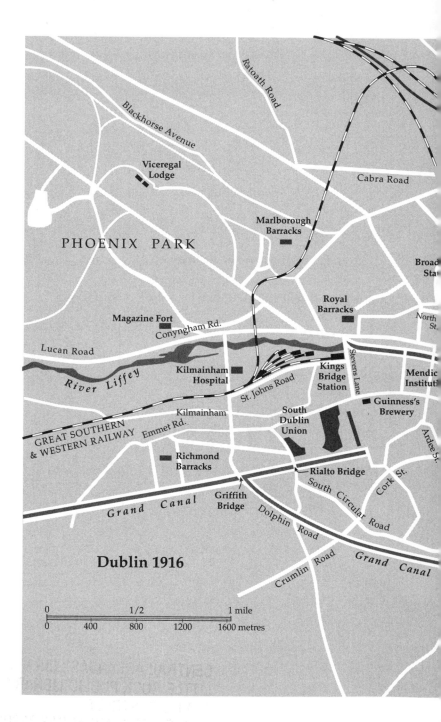

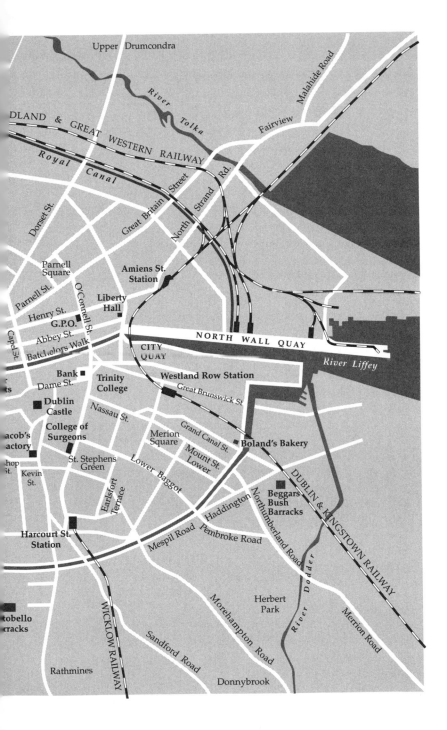

POLITICAL BACKGROUND
TO THE RISING

1913

31 January: Formation of the Ulster Volunteer Force in response to the threat of Home Rule for Ireland.

26 August: Start of the Dublin Lock-Out. Strike by Dublin tram workers belonging to the Irish Transport and General Workers Union (ITGWU) begins, and develops into general lock-out of workers by Dublin employers.

19 November: Formation of the Irish Citizen Army (ICA) to protect strikers, under the leadership of union-organiser James Connolly and with the strong support of rebel Ascendancy heiress Countess Markievicz.

25 November: Formation of the Irish Volunteers, with Eoin MacNeill as Chief of Staff. MacNeill is Professor of History at University College Dublin and founder member of the Gaelic League. The Volunteers include members of nationalist organisations such as the Gaelic League, the Ancient Order of Hibernians and Sinn Féin. The organisation is dedicated to safeguarding Home Rule but is infiltrated by members of the secret, oath-bound revolutionary organisation the Irish Republican Brotherhood (IRB), whose aim is the establishment of an Irish Republic.

1914

March–June: The nationalist Irish Parliamentary Party,
   under leader John Redmond, effectively takes control
   of the Irish Volunteers by insisting on Redmond's
   appointments to the ruling executive committee.
2 April: Formation of Cumann na mBan, women's auxiliary
   to the Irish Volunteers.
24–6: Larne gun-running. The Ulster Volunteer Force
   smuggles 25,000 German rifles and two million rounds
   of ammunition on two ships into Larne, in preparation
   for the 'defence' of Ulster if Home Rule becomes law.
July: Membership of the Irish Volunteers peaks at 150,000–
   180,000 members.
26 July: Howth gun-running. Fifteen hundred German
   rifles landed at Howth for the Volunteers. Later that day
   the British army fire on civilians in Dublin's Bachelor's
   Walk and four civilians are killed.
3 August: Outbreak of the First World War.
18 September: Government of Ireland Act, 1914, receives
   Royal Assent. The Act allowing for the introduction of
   Home Rule to Ireland is placed on the statute books, but
   delayed for a year because of the war.
20 September: John Redmond, leader of the Irish
   Parliamentary Party, pledges the support of the Irish
   Volunteers in the war, in the interests of ensuring the
   implementation of Home Rule.
24 September: Split in the Irish Volunteers. The
   overwhelming majority (an estimated 90 per cent)
   of the Irish Volunteers leave the organisation and
   join the National Volunteers, under John Redmond.
   This organisation is pledged to support the war. The
   minority Irish Volunteers remain under the leadership

of Eoin MacNeill. There is some overlap in membership between the Irish Volunteers and the political organisation led by Arthur Griffith, Sinn Féin, but the two organisations are separate.

1915

Spring: The Supreme Council of the Irish Republican Brotherhood forms a military committee to plan an uprising before the end of the war. The committee includes Patrick Pearse, Éamonn Ceannt, Joseph Plunkett, Sean MacDermott and Thomas Clarke. All except Clarke are members of the Irish Volunteers, but Eoin MacNeill, leader of the Irish Volunteers, is unaware of the IRB plot. Joseph Plunkett travels to Germany to negotiate German aid for a rising in Ireland.

1916

January: James Connolly, head of the Irish Citizen Army, is unaware of the IRB's plans for a rising. He threatens to start a rebellion through the ICA. The leaders of the IRB meet with Connolly and agree on a joint rising at Easter. Connolly joins the Military Committee of the IRB. (The seventh signatory of the Proclamation of the Republic, Thomas MacDonagh, will join later that spring.)
3 April: Patrick Pearse issues orders for large-scale manoeuvres of the Volunteers to begin on Easter Sunday. The Rising is set to take place under cover of the manoeuvres. The German ship the *Aud* sets sail for Kerry, loaded with arms. Sir Roger Casement returns to

Ireland on a German U-boat in an attempt to persuade
the leaders of the Rising to call it off.

20 April: Eoin MacNeill hears of the planned Rising and
is briefly persuaded by Sean MacDermott to support it
when he is told of the shipment of German arms.

Good Friday, 21 April: MacNeill hears that the shipment
of arms has been scuttled after interception by the
British navy, and that Casement has been arrested in
County Kerry. He issues a countermand, printed in
the newspapers of 23 April, cancelling the manoeuvres
planned for the following day. The British authorities
decide to arrest the leaders of the plot but postpone
action until after Easter Monday.

Easter Sunday night, 23 April: The military leaders decide
to strike the following day. The Proclamation of the
Republic is printed on Sunday night at Liberty Hall,
offices of the ITGWU and headquarters of the ICA.
The seven signatories to the Proclamation:

Thomas J. Clarke, a veteran of the IRB who had served
fifteen years in prison for his part in a dynamiting
campaign in London in the 1880s.

Seán Mac Diarmada (Sean MacDermott), a leading
member of the IRB and close friend of Clarke.
MacDermott was imprisoned during 1915 for making
seditious speeches.

Thomas MacDonagh, a poet, dramatist and lecturer
in English at University College Dublin. MacDonagh
joined the Irish Volunteers in 1913 and the IRB in 1915.

P. H. Pearse, a poet and teacher, headmaster of St Enda's
School, a member of the IRB since 1913 and a founding
member of the Irish Volunteers. By 1915 Pearse was the

Director of Military Organization for the Irish Volunteers
and a member of the IRB's Military Committee.
Éamonn Ceannt, a member of the IRB since 1913 and a
founding member of the Irish Volunteers.
James Connolly, socialist, trades unionist and leader of
the Irish Citizen Army.
Joseph Plunkett, a poet and co-founder in 1914 of the
Irish Theatre Company with Thomas MacDonagh (and
Edward Martyn). Plunkett was an early member of the
Irish Volunteers and joined the IRB in 1915, when he was
quickly co-opted to the IRB Military Committee.
All the signatories except MacDonagh and Ceannt will
be based in the GPO during Easter week.

Easter Monday, 24 April: The Rising begins, but with
reduced numbers because of MacNeill's countermanding order. It is for the most part confined to
Dublin, where rebels take over strategic buildings and
hold out for up to a week, though there are also actions
in Galway, Wexford and Meath.

29 April: Pearse issues the order for surrender, which is
upheld by Connolly for the men and women of the Irish
Citizen Army.

2 May: A series of courts martial begins, following mass
arrests, and ninety people are sentenced to death.

3–12 May: Execution of the leaders. Fifteen men, including
the seven signatories to the Proclamation of the
Republic, are executed by firing squad.

3 August: Sir Roger Casement is hanged in London.

Introduction

IN THE NAME OF GOD
AND OF THE DEAD GENERATIONS

If we still dwelled among our memories there would be no need to consecrate sites embodying them.

Pierre Nora

In the name of God and of the dead generations from which she receives her old tradition of nationhood, Ireland, through us, summons her children to her flag and strikes for her freedom ... In every generation the Irish people have asserted their right to national freedom and sovereignty: six times during the past three hundred years they have asserted it in arms. Standing on that fundamental right and again asserting it in arms in the face of the world, we hereby proclaim the Irish Republic as a Sovereign Independent State, and we pledge our lives and the lives of our comrades-in-arms to the cause of its freedom, of its welfare, and of its exaltation among the nations.

Proclamation of the Republic, 1916

On Easter Monday, 24 April 1916, while large crowds of Dubliners were at the seaside or at the horse races at Fairyhouse, a group of Irish Volunteers, led by members of the secret revolutionary organisation the Irish Republican Brother-hood, and 200 members of the socialist Irish Citizen Army, assembled at Liberty Hall in the centre of Dublin. A nation-wide armed uprising against British rule planned for the previous day had been called off in confusion, but some of the leaders of the rebel faction had decided to continue with the rising in Dublin, and to seize a number of key locations in the city. These included the General Post Office (which would become the headquarters of the rebellion), the Four Courts, St Stephen's Green and strategic buildings such as Boland's Mill and Jacob's Biscuit Factory, as well as the roads controlling entry to the city from the nearby port. Held for a week by the rebels, the buildings were finally surrendered to the Crown forces after heavy gun bombardment, and the conflagration caused by incendiary bombs, turned the GPO into an empty shell and destroyed much of the centre of the city.

The 1916 Rising is seen as the most significant single event in modern Ireland, or, as one historian has put it, 'the point of departure ... for all subsequent Irish history'. Six years later, following a protracted War of Independence, the Anglo-Irish Treaty gave partial independence to the Irish Free State. But the treaty was contested, and ushered in a bloody and divisive civil war. The events of Easter week, by contrast, could command allegiance from both sides of the nationalist divide. The GPO very quickly became the most famous building in Ireland, and it has been the focus of national parades, celebrations and commemorations over the past century.

The legacy of the Rising has never been uncontested, however. It has been claimed as the founding act of the democratic Irish state. As the country consolidated its

1. An engraving, from the early 1820s, by G. H. Jones, of the new Post Office in Sackville Street which opened in 1818. Even allowing for the absence of modern street furniture and traffic, the perspective emphasises the width of the street and heightens the grandeur of the building.

independence the Easter commemorations at the GPO became the equivalent of Independence Day in America or Bastille Day in France, culminating in the lavish fiftieth-anniversary celebrations orchestrated on a scale resembling nothing so much as the Coronation of Elizabeth II. Yet there were always those who argued that the Rising was a sectarian, violent putsch by an unelected group, a bloody rebellion against a democratically elected government. As war returned to the North the wisdom of celebrating armed insurrection came increasingly into question, and the official GPO parades were discontinued.

An event that foreshadowed some of the century's major conflicts, which laid down a new model of urban insurrection, and reconfigured the relationship between politics and literature, the Rising has never been far from modern political consciousness – and not only in Ireland. Erupting in the middle of the Great War, the Rising put the issue of national and imperial allegiance sharply into focus, and its legacy was felt in anti-imperial movements throughout the first half of the twentieth century. But it also helped to shape our understanding of the links between socialism and revolutionary action. The nature of heroism, the problems of pacifism and militarism, the place for personal bravery and idealism in the pursuit of political goals, the role of literature in creating, responding to and helping to define political events – the terms of all these debates were transformed by what happened in Easter week.

The Rising was intended to be world-historical from the start. It was staged as an event in revolutionary history. The Proclamation of the Republic harked back to the French Revolution – as did the language of barricades, and the new 'revolutionary' calendar: Easter Monday 1916 was hailed as the '1st Day of the Republic'. While contemporary commentators wrote that all eyes were on the GPO, inside the building the epoch-making nature of the event was emphasised not only by the telegraphed messages to the world, and the printed messages to the citizens of Dublin, but by the rebels' own consciousness that they were making history. One apocryphal story has it that as O'Connell Street blazed, Joseph Plunkett, one of the leaders, remarked it was the first time a capital city had burned since Moscow. The GPO was transformed into a national monument even before the Rising was half over.

At the heart of the Rising lay the declaration of independence, but there was more at stake than a protest against British rule. The leaders of the Rising were also proclaiming a new type of politics. The men who planned it were inspired by radical (and sometimes contradictory) social and political ideals such as socialism, women's suffrage, the Irish language movement and even progressive education. Famously a revolution led by poets (Patrick Pearse, Joseph Plunkett and Thomas MacDonagh had all published poems and plays), it was also led by political idealists. James Connolly was a Labour leader who had formed the Irish Citizen Army to protect workers during the 1913 Lock-Out, when big business had tried to break the unions. The Rising has been hailed as the world's first anti-colonial revolt, a spur for anti-colonial movements throughout the world. The successful guerrilla campaign by the IRA after the First World War may have provided a guide for the later wars of liberation in Palestine, or Nicaragua, or Vietnam. Far earlier, Marcus Garvey and black nationalist revolutionaries hailed the Rising as inspiration for their movement. Garvey named the Universal Negro Improvement Association general meeting place 'Liberty Hall', after the headquarters of the Irish Citizen Army. The Chittagong Uprising in Bengal, in 1930, was explicitly modelled on the Easter Rising, even down to the decision to carry out the raid at Easter – surely not the most obvious choice for a primarily Hindu rebellion. Others have suggested (with far less cause) analogies with Mussolini's March on Rome and Hitler's Munich Putsch.

Why the GPO? There has been keen speculation over why the rebel leaders selected the GPO rather than, for example, Dublin Castle, as their headquarters. Beyond the practicalities (the Castle would have been far harder to take, and to keep), was there a symbolic dimension to the choice of the GPO? The Post Office was one of the most well-established institutions in Ireland, an arm of the civil service dedicated

2. *A photograph of the refurbished interior of the GPO, which re-opened for business only six weeks before the Rising. The photograph was published in the* Irish Builder and Engineer *in April 1916, and as one of the few images of the public office before its destruction it has guided later reconstructions.*

to postal, banking and – by 1916 – telephone and telegraph services. The building itself was one of the most imposing in Dublin. Designed by Francis Johnston, and opened in 1818, its three-storey granite sweep, its stately Ionic columns, and classical statues (Mercury, Fidelity and Hibernia) staring out on Nelson's Pillar, were emblems of post-Trafalgar imperial confidence on a scale at odds with the city streets around it. The massive structure had recently received a twentieth-century makeover. Hamilton Norway, the new Secretary of the Post Office, who took over in 1912, poured money into refurbishing the building to render it fit for the Empire's second city. The newly designed Public Office, accessed for the first time through the grand central doors under the

3. The 'Telephone Silence Cabinet', a centrepiece of the public office in the new GPO. In the first hours of the Rising a British soldier who had been buying stamps when the building was stormed was placed inside the box with his hands tied.

portico, was opened only six weeks before the Rising began. As the Secretary's wife recalled:

> It was really beautiful. The roof was a large glass dome, with elaborate plaster work, beautiful white pillars,

mosaic floor, counters all of red teak wood, and bright brass fittings everywhere – a public building of which any city might be proud; and in six weeks all that is left is a smoking heap of ashes.

For all its splendour, the GPO lacked the martial signifi-cance of Dublin Castle. It was a symbol of commercial rather than military power, and it had a very different standing with the Irish public. It was situated in the heart of the com-mercial district, yet surrounded by slums. The GPO portico was used as shelter by Dublin's shoppers but also by the city's prostitutes. It stood for control but it was also where you bought your stamps. The building managed to function simultaneously as a symbol of empire and of a quotidian aspect of Dublin life, and this dual status, as linchpin in the presentation of the state – whether British or Irish – and at the same time owned by the ordinary citizen, has marked the story of the GPO ever since.

Long before the Rising, O'Connell Street itself was a locus for nationalist protest. From the turn of the century, the urban landscape in Dublin had become intensely politi-cised. The unusual width of the street, busy with shoppers and travellers waiting for trams, offered maximum expo-sure to anyone seeking to draw attention to themselves – an ideal arena for Home Rule protests, Gaelic League demon-strations, labour agitation and housing campaigns. During the Boer War, O'Connell Street had been the site of a drive against Irish enlistment in the British army, orchestrated by nationalist women, including Maud Gonne. Women gath-ering under the GPO portico were targeted with leaflets asking them not to consort with British soldiers, while the soldiers themselves were followed inside the saloons by leaflet-toting middle-class women. With nationalist street performances like this, along with the speeches and parades, it is easy to see why the GPO might have appeared as the perfect backdrop for a Rising dependent on visibility – on flags and proclamations as well as on armed men – for its success. By storming a working monument, neither Castle nor Bastille, but a building devoted to communications, the leaders of the Irish Rising became the forerunners of the modern coup. The rebels took over what would now be the television station.

In the early years of the Irish Free State the events which took place in and around the GPO in 1916 achieved the status of founding myth for the nation. It is perhaps not surprising, then, that the symbolic importance of the building has been repeatedly read back into the events of Easter week itself. In historical accounts, reconstructions and commemorations, the building has figured as a major character in the story of the rebellion. Episode Six of RTÉ's landmark 1966 television series *Insurrection* ended with Patrick Pearse taking a last long look at the burning building, as though by Friday of Easter week it was already a sacred site. Eoin Ó Súilleabháin, the actor playing Pearse, lingered so long to watch with reverence as the set collapsed around him that his hair and eyebrows were singed.

Mad as it was to suggest that the rebels would endanger themselves by genuflecting to bricks and mortar, the veneration of the building did set in early. One eyewitness to the Rising implied that ordinary citizens grasped the significance of the GPO even before events had sealed it: 'Upon that building the minds and tongues of the whole city ran during the anxious hours. The *fons et origo* of the passionate dream, its fate stood for the fate of the whole adventure.'

Some stories about the Rising even read the conflagration of the GPO back into the original intention of the rebels, such as this poem about rebel leader Thomas Clarke, who owned a tobacconist shop around the corner from the GPO on Parnell Street:

As evening falls in Dublin
And the twilight gathers round Parnell Street
I have visions of a quiet man
Looking and gazing at the Post Office, distant some
    hundred feet
So he must have waited, so have been his desire
To send word out of that building
To awaken Ireland with a house on fire.

The idea that Clarke and his fellow insurrectionists had planned all along to be burnt out of the Post Office is a superb piece of hindsight, but it has a certain neatness – as though the rebels had orchestrated their own near immolation so that phoenix-like from the flames a new political and civil dispensation might spring.

There were European, classical and Christian analogies (not least the story of Easter sacrifice), but the principal historical precedent for the insurrection was Ireland's revolutionary past. The Proclamation of the Republic, read in front of the GPO on Easter Monday, insisted on the obligation of the generation of 1916 to the dead generations of revolutionaries, and the legitimacy conferred by those past generations on the present. Six times in the last 300 years the Irish had risen against their colonial oppressors. The rebels evoked the battles of the Irish Rebellion of 1641, the Jacobite War beginning in 1689, the United Irishmen rebellion of 1798, Robert

Emmet's rebellion of 1803, the 1848 Young Ireland Rebellion and the Fenian Rising of 1867. The Easter Rising was itself a commemoration, a re-enactment of a recurring need. The signatories to the Proclamation were declaring the duty owed to dead generations of revolutionaries to carry on the fight. But at the same time they were claiming strength for their own generation. A generation is a product of memory, but in this case it was also an aspiration – the Army of the Republic wanted to become the new generation, wrapping round themselves the symbolic mantle that the word 'generation' confers, in which a few can stand for the many. By living up to the past, they would transform the grubby and debased present, in which the ideal of national sovereignty had been lost.

In this play with generation and youth the rebels were evoking another model – the generation of young men who took part in the First World War. The leaders of the Rising were far from young (Thomas Clarke was fifty-nine), but commentators repeatedly emphasised the extreme youth of the rebels ('there were guns pointing out of the GPO and youths of 15 or 16 behind each of them'), while the rebels themselves commented on how the British Tommies seemed mere boys. Much of the fighting in the city had been planned with a shadowy idea of trench warfare in mind – the barricades and static siege tactics were, if not consciously, an urban version of the stalemate in the trenches. In so many ways the rebellion mirrored the war it opposed – the fear of gas attacks, the digging of trenches, the shelling and heavy gun bombardment, but also the public school rhetoric of nobility and honour, and the exaltation of violence.

The Rising turned on a question of legitimacy, of who had the right to speak on behalf of the Irish people. After the death of Parnell the Irish Parliamentary Party seemed to have lost its way. With Home Rule legislation on the statute books, but shelved on the outbreak of war, the leader of the Irish Parliamentary Party, John Redmond, had pledged the support of the Irish Volunteers in Britain's war with Germany, on the promise that Home Rule would be implemented at war's end. This provoked a split in the Volunteer movement and – in the long run – allowed the 'advanced nationalists' to take control of the movement in Ireland and to plan the Rising.

The rebels themselves, for the most part, understood their fight in terms of national self-determination. The principal issue was the takeover of political power. They were claiming the same rights for Ireland as for other European nations, conceived in the mould of nineteenth-century theories of national distinction rather than anti-colonial liberation. The idea of the Republic for the majority of the rebels meant not a radical social programme but national sovereignty.

Indeed, for a great many of the volunteers, republicanism meant simply physical force as opposed to constitutional means of gaining independence. It did not even necessarily imply a particular form of government. Inside the GPO the rebels discussed the merits and demerits of inviting the German prince Joachim, youngest son of Kaiser Wilhelm II, to become monarch, in the confident belief that within a few generations of intermarriage the Royal Family would become truly Irish. This kind of ideological confusion led some of the leaders of international socialism to dismiss the Rising as a mere bourgeois putsch, lacking the ingredients – and the popular support – necessary for real transformation. Lenin disagreed. He argued that the broad spectrum of opinion brought together in the Rising made it a truly 'social revolution'. The insurgents' only problem was that they rose too early.

What might have happened had they waited – until the disillusion with the world war became more widespread, until conscription was threatened in Ireland in 1918, until after the Russian Revolution, until demobbed soldiers returned to Ireland? All of these shifts may well have resulted in greater backing for the rebels. As it was, the Rising that went ahead on Easter Monday, in defiance of the cancellation order from the Chief of Staff of the Irish Volunteers, Eoin MacNeill (concerned about the loss of a shipment of German arms, and convinced that a rising could only be justified if the British attempted to suppress the Volunteers) did not garner much popular support. The rebels hoped their action would galvanise the public into action. Pearse called on the citizens of Dublin for assistance: 'Citizens can help the Republican forces by building barricades in the streets to impede the advance of the British troops. Up with the Barricades!' The insurgents trapped in the GPO were heartened by rumours that the rest of the country was rising. But it was not until after the execution of the leaders that the tide of support turned in favour of the rebels.

Even before the end of Easter week the leaders were describing the Rising as a symbolic sacrifice for the nation, rather than as a military enterprise. The last bulletin written by Pearse inside the GPO was full of the language of noble sacrifice for 'Ireland's honour':

> Each individual has spent himself, happy to pour out his strength for Ireland and for Freedom. If they do not win this fight, they will at least have deserved to win it. But win it they will, although they may win it in

death. Already they have won a great thing. They have redeemed Dublin from many shames, and made her name splendid among the names of Cities.

What else could he say? The idea of the Rising as the courageous stand of citizens redeeming the nation from shame was copper-fastened by the execution of the leaders. A kind of martyrology very quickly grew up around the dead leaders, emphasising their saintliness and their courage in the face of death. A flood of relic-like ephemera swamped the streets of Dublin – Mass cards, ballad sheets, last words, pictures of the scene inside the GPO, postcards, character sketches, poems, tricolours, Easter lilies. On the night before his execution Sean MacDermott cut the buttons off his tunic to give as relics to his friends.

The notion that the leaders, and the rebels who had died during Easter week, had willingly sacrificed themselves for the nation set in train a process of codifying the story of the Rising itself as a mythic and symbolic event, rather than as a military undertaking. Though much of this reverence was couched in the terms of pious Catholicism, at its heart lay a much more basic admiration for a bunch of men who had had the guts to stand up to the might of the British Empire. As Jawaharlal Nehru put it in his prison cell in 1935, 'The Easter week rising in Ireland by its very failure attracted. For was that not true courage which mocked at almost certain failure and proclaimed to the world that no physical might could crush the invincible spirit of a nation?' It was in that year that the statue of the dying mythic Irish hero Cuchulainn was unveiled in the GPO, completing the transformation of the building into a temple – the classical pillars did nothing to discourage its identification as a place of para-religious worship of the spirit of the nation.

This mythic version of events – at its heart the morally courageous and chivalrous rebel – coexisted with a contradictory impulse towards absolute verisimilitude, a detailed documentary account of what happened in and around the GPO. There was of course no necessary conflict between the myth of glorious and heroic deeds and the detailed reports by participants – participants increasingly wished to further the aura of heroism. Indeed the instant publishing of diaries and eyewitness accounts, the more literary the better, quickly became part of the event itself. Nonetheless the impulse to gather accurate testimony, the obsession with the meticulous reconstruction of events, sat uneasily with the mythic and symbolic value of the Rising. There was an uncomfortable gap between the two sorts of accounts, not least because the tale of gallant sacrifice had little room for the chaos, confusion or fear experienced by individuals caught up in the violence.

In the run-up to the twentieth anniversary of the Rising one volunteer, Diarmuid Lynch (a member of the Irish Republican Brotherhood), undertook to gather first-hand information on the events in the GPO from all the people who were there, in order to construct the definitive narrative of Easter week in the GPO. He sent his questionnaire to more than 180 men and women and their replies now lie in a dusty metal box in the National Library in Dublin. The correspondence is a jigsaw of exquisite detail: what individual insurgents did, what they saw, what they ate and, on occasion, what they felt. Lynch spent months and in some cases years verifying details, writing back to participants asking them to draw the precise shape of the sloping roof, the exact location of outposts, the particular routes taken in and out of the building. When written correspondence failed to clear up certain details, he held meetings on site to verify the facts. He then gathered the whole garrison together to read his account to them, and revised it accordingly. Yet the narrative that Lynch based on this cornucopia of detail is a model of abstraction. He edited out the chaos, and so too the individual experiences on which the larger story of the GPO is based. His account betrays all the marks of having to measure up to a grand design, not only that of glorious deeds, but of military order and efficiency.

Lynch's questionnaire was simply one of a very large number of attempts to tell the 'true' story of the GPO. From early newspaper accounts, to first-hand reports published in sympathetic journals, to anniversary recollections, to the official Witness Statements collected by the Irish Bureau of Military History in the 1940s and 1950s, to later histories, novels and plays, the debate about what went on in the GPO has been a battle between history and memory. The obsessive, almost photographic detail that was a defining feature of the participant accounts was partly about needing to prove they were there. But as the years passed, memories persisted only when they were corroborated by others – and indeed memories were created in this way, like remembering events from childhood that you never saw. So that although there were more than 400 insurgents in the GPO at different times during Easter week, the memories of events narrowed to a few 'shared' moments. Individuals increasingly had memories of things that had happened to other people, particularly the leaders, or of events that could be seen from a number of different vantage points, so they could be confirmed by others. An odd consequence of this is that we know more about what happened in the street (which could be seen from all sides) than inside the building.

The construction of a shared GPO story went along with the literal reconstruction of the burnt-out building, a place where the past could be held, and visited. 'What stalked through the Post Office?' asked W. B. Yeats, and one answer was the national inspiration for future generations. The Rising looked simultaneously forward and back. Just as the rebels drew legitimacy from the past, so Pearse insisted that the present must take its meaning from the future: the rebels' willing sacrifice of their lives, he confidently predicted, would bear fruit. Throughout the middle years of the twentieth century, that guilty sense of being the fruit of sacrifice dominated approaches to the Rising. For many years GPO commemorations showcased the spirit of the nation through the veterans of the Rising. As the years passed their ageing faces simultaneously revealed what was being lost as the new state developed, and (particularly in the 1960s, when television lent close-ups of the veterans' faces a kind of hieratic aura) the spirit that remained. So it was the youth of the country that was called on to embody that spirit in a kind of yearly political vegetation ceremony. On countless Easter Sundays, at parades and even at family gatherings, pre-adolescent children read the Proclamation of the Republic to the assembled elders.

Now there are no veterans left, and the building has passed decisively out of the realm of memory and experience and into that of national heritage. An essential stop on the tourist trail, the GPO signifies Irishness in much the same way as Celtic symbols or the landscape of the western seaboard. It is a commonplace that heritage sites codify the past for the purposes of the present – the processes of modernisation send us back to the past, but a past remade for the present. Our nostalgic longing for the aura of the past is a consequence not of continuity but of rupture. The postmodern Rising kitsch that adorns many Irish homes may look like the relics and memorabilia which flooded Dublin in the weeks and months after the event in 1916, but it has been emptied of the reverential, quasi-sacred significance of the earlier moment.

Yet at the beginning of 2006, the ninetieth anniversary year, President Mary McAleese opened discussion of the legacy of the Rising by asserting its contemporary relevance:

> Like every nation that had to wrench its freedom from the reluctant grip of empire, we have our idealistic and heroic founding fathers and mothers – our Davids to their Goliaths. The small band who proclaimed the Rising inhabited a sea of death, an unspeakable time of the most profligate world-wide waste of human life. Yet their deaths rise far above the clamour – their voices, insistent still.

Invoking the rebels who fought and died in 1916 as part of Ireland's contemporary social landscape appears at first glance to be a throwback to the nationalist rhetoric of the early years of independence, of days long before the Celtic Tiger and the Peace Process. In the iconography of what it means to be Irish in the early twenty-first century – creative, entrepreneurial, economically successful, relatively European and just a little bit Celtic – a starring role for the building associated with armed insurrection against British rule seems unlikely. In most other respects Irish citizens seem happy to turn their backs on the history of 'nationalist struggle'.

The lavish ninetieth-anniversary celebrations were part

and parcel of the Irish government's concerted efforts to reclaim the legacy of 1916 from dissident republicans, and from Sinn Féin. Yet the thousands who turned out to watch the reinstated Easter parade in 2006 suggests that whatever meanings the building holds, it does so beyond manipulation by a political elite. Indeed the GPO is the favourite site not only of official commemorations, but of unofficial public protest. The first choice for demonstrations on a whole raft of national and international issues such as extraordinary rendition, Chinese policy in Tibet, Irish abortion laws and the war in Iraq, the building occupies a place in the Irish public consciousness somewhere between the Palace of Westminster, the White House and the Place de la Bastille. It is a platform for speaking to the nation.

Like the revamped state Easter parades, contemporary invocations of the GPO reveal a profound alteration in Ireland's relationship to its past and to traditional forms of Irish national sentiment. Rather than using the Rising to legitimise or criticise the political status quo – as governments and their opponents have done throughout the century – today a confident, pluralist society confers legitimacy on the Rising. For while nations may need legitimisation from the past, society does not. The centennial of the Rising in 2016 will see the culmination of a process that has already begun, in which the achievements of modern Ireland – a self-confident, outward-looking and increasingly diverse nation – are claimed as the original impetus behind the rebels' actions.

What is lost in this process is a sense of the otherness of the past. The men and women involved in the event and its aftermath were caught up in idealism and forms of violence that took their meaning from the rhetoric and experience of the First World War, and from nineteenth-century ideas of nationhood, which are hard for us to understand today. Yet alongside the transformation of the Rising into a bland, twenty-first-century version of itself, the GPO continues to figure in Irish popular consciousness in recalcitrant ways. The reluctance of many of the citizens of Dublin to allow it to be turned into a museum or a shopping centre is one index of the Rising's ability to maintain an imaginative hold on the public, outside of the orchestrations of governments. Meanwhile the tussle over the political and cultural legacy of the Rising – socialist, capitalist, anti-British, anti-colonial, anti-democratic, sectarian – is still being played out at the GPO.

Although this book will take account of the political history of the Rising, its focus is on the events of Easter week, and on the symbolism of the events and their aftermath. I concentrate on the transformation of the GPO from an emblem of nineteenth-century British power and civil government to a barricade against shelling, to a national symbol. What did it feel like to be trapped inside the building? What was it like to watch, and listen to, the destruction of the city? Was it intended as a bloody sacrifice or a military coup d'état? I explore the revisions and re-imaginings of the GPO by architects, writers, artists, politicians and revolutionaries. The book moves from the drama of the events inside the building to the drama of representation – in parades, plays, poems and politics.

But I also examine the meanings of the GPO beyond its place in a national story. Commentators at the time wondered whether it was the beginning of a 'French Revolution' in Britain and Ireland. One of the reasons the building has continued to hold our attention is precisely because of its ambivalence – at once an archaic gesture of symbolic defiance against the British Empire (the allegory of Easter; the

images of celt and sword), a prototype of the modern coup
and a model for popular insurgence. During the nineteenth
century, Irish anti-colonial agitation had been a rural affair, a
conflict between landlord and tenant, and a matter of secret
societies. The occupation of the GPO by uniformed men,
who spoke the language of battalion and garrison, brought
secret organisation, modern soldiering and urban warfare
together in new ways. As a correspondent for the *Irish
Builder* wrote in May 1916, the city had been put through
'a period of thrills, alarms and horrors more closely associated with the South American Republics than with a sane
and prosperous nation'.

1

OCCUPATION

AMAL: *Say, what's going on there in that big house on the other side, where there is a flag flying high up, and the people are always going in and out?*
WATCHMAN: *Oh, there? That's our new Post Office.*
AMAL: *Post Office? Whose?*
WATCHMAN: *Whose? Why, the King's surely!*
> Rabindranath Tagore, *The Post Office: A Play*, (1914)

Yet their descendants, if they grow rich enough for the travel and leisure that make a finished man, will constitute our ruling class, and date their origins from the Post Office as American families date theirs from the Mayflower.
> W. B. Yeats, *On the Boiler* (1938)

Halfway through ten o'clock Mass on Easter Monday morning, Máire nic Shiubhlaigh's father tapped on her shoulder – a telegram had come from her friend Lily O'Brennan: 'Come at once.' She sidled out of church and dashed into town, but when she got to O'Connell Street she had trouble getting on to a southbound tram. 'There was a long wait at the Pillar. The city was thronged with bank holiday crowds and racegoers making the best of the warm weather. Crowds heaved and pushed under the porticoes of the GPO. Long queues lined the street to the tram stops. At the O'Connell Bridge junction, traffic was held up by a stream of cyclists.' She got through eventually and was posted to Jacob's Biscuit Factory, where she spent the days preparing food for the garrison. Later that week she would climb to the roof of the factory in order to watch 'the last of the burning GPO'.

Nic Shiubhlaigh's account of the 1916 Rising is framed by these contrasting visions of the building, even though she was based elsewhere all week. This reverent nod to the GPO is replicated in scores of accounts by participants and onlookers, and even in the official British records. In 1918 *The Times History of the War* argued that the GPO had been a good choice for military headquarters. The building was 'not badly chosen, seeing that the Post Office is, or rather was, an isolated, powerfully-constructed stone building, and commands the main street of the city. It was also the meeting place of the wires and cables that control electric communications all over Ireland and to England.'

Those wires and cables were humming. Despite the crowds heaving under the portico, the bank holiday didn't mean a day off for all staff – they had handled Máire nic Shiubhlaigh's telegram, for a start. There were girls at work in the telegraph room on the second floor; guards were posted inside the building, even though, as it turned out, they had no ammunition for their guns; there were tellers selling stamps and manning the different counters in the public office; Hamilton Norway, the Secretary of the Post Office, was at work in his office upstairs until about 11.45, when he walked over to Dublin Castle for a meeting – about the security situation – with the Under-Secretary for Ireland, Sir Matthew Nathan. What happened in his absence has been recounted so often it has the status of myth. At midday,

Patrick Pearse, James Connolly and Joseph Plunkett marched from Liberty Hall, the headquarters of the Citizen Army, through Abbey Street and up O'Connell Street to the GPO. They had with them about 150 men, armed with an assortment of weapons, who at Connolly's command charged at the building. Most of them stuffed themselves through the front doors, though about a dozen ran up the stairs at the Henry Street entrance in order to secure the upper storeys.

Early accounts by those sympathetic to the rebels liked to stress the order, calm and efficiency which reigned in the GPO all week, proving that this was no mere riot but the action of dedicated Volunteers. Those who succumbed to hysteria or funk were usually identified as British prisoners or civilians. But the story of smooth operations conducted by unruffled soldiers is hard to maintain in relation to these first chaotic hours. The first difficulty faced by the insurgents was the unwillingness of the Post Office staff and their customers to take them at all seriously. As Volunteers jumped across the counters and shouted 'Hands Up', customers responded with irritation rather than respect for armed might. No doubt this was partly because the Volunteers themselves were only slowly beginning to realise that this was for real. Eventually Connolly fired in the air to show he meant business, and the building was evacuated, though the crowds continued to peer in at the windows.

Upstairs there was a ruckus when the men detailed to take over the instrument room tussled with guards. The Post Office workers quickly piled chairs and boxes into the corridor at the northern end of the room, but the O'Rahilly hopped round to the door at the other end, where he encountered no resistance. A founding member of the Irish Volunteers, the O'Rahilly had not been party to the secret plans

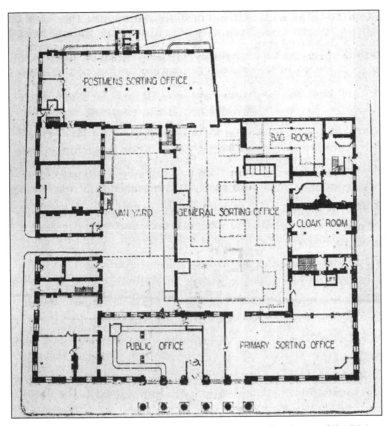

4. *Ground floor plan of the refurbished GPO. In the first hours of the Rising the partitions between the public office and sorting offices were torn down, and a field hospital was established to the rear of the building. The van yard led out onto Prince's St and the Henry St entrance was on the right near the bag room.*

of the revolutionary faction. When he heard of the planned Rising the week before Easter, he was initially opposed to the idea and had spent much of Easter Saturday driving round the country to call off Sunday's mobilisation; but on Easter

Monday he arrived at Liberty Hall, reluctantly prepared to join the rebels. He entered the telegraph room at the GPO pointing his pistol and saying something like, 'This is the first and last act.' Nonetheless, some of the women operating the telegraph machines initially refused to leave. Meanwhile, men were ordered to man the roof and to take up guard at sentry posts on all floors of the building. Those on the ground floor had the most work to do, smashing all the windows, building barricades, demolishing the partitions between the sorting rooms, readying the building for an imminent attack. In one area on the ground floor, members of Cumann na mBan, the women's auxiliary force of the Volunteers, began to set up a field hospital. Upstairs, Desmond FitzGerald – another Volunteer officer who had not been in on the secret plans for the Rising and who therefore arrived a little late – took command of the kitchens, setting the women to work on preparing food, and filling as many containers as possible with water, to be ranged along the corridors in case of fire.

Sean T. O'Kelly, future President of Ireland, arrived at the GPO just after the occupation and found he had to push his way in. 'I eventually found myself in a room upstairs with Tom Clarke, Sean MacDermott and Joe Plunkett, who was stretched out on a mattress on the floor.' (Plunkett had just been released from hospital, and was to spend much of the week recovering from an operation for glandular tuberculosis.) Officers were stationing men all over the building, but O'Kelly was sent back to Liberty Hall by James Connolly to get flags out of 'the press' in a room at the back. The tricolour and a green flag embroidered with the words 'Irish Republic' and apparently designed by the Countess Markievicz were run up on the roof of the GPO; the Plough and the Stars, the flag of the Irish Citizen Army, was hoisted on the roof of the Imperial Hotel opposite. Pearse and Connolly emerged from the GPO to read the now famous Proclamation declaring the establishment of an Irish Republic to a mostly bemused and indifferent crowd of onlookers. Rumours were that the Germans had landed.

Over the next twenty-four hours the rebels fortified the building, using walls of Post Office notebooks, among other things, to build bullet-proof defences. They took over surrounding buildings, knocking through cellars and walls to create tunnels between them; they constructed street barricades from shop fittings and merchandise (hundreds of bicycles, scores of marble clocks). Meanwhile, across the city, groups of insurgents were taking up other positions: the young Fianna boy scouts, the youth wing of the Volunteers, dug trenches in Stephen's Green under the command of Countess Markievicz; a group holed up in Jacob's Biscuit Factory; and the future Taoiseach Eamon de Valera established his men in Boland's Mill. All these positions were nominally under the command of Headquarters at the GPO.

Yet this was hardly going according to plan. For months the small group of revolutionaries in the secret organisation the Irish Republican Brotherhood had worked on ambitious plans for a rising of the Irish Volunteers in the west, assisted by German arms landed at Fenit in County Kerry, and a simultaneous takeover of the centre of Dublin. Early in 1916 James Connolly and the Irish Citizen Army had been brought into the conspiracy. The date was set for Easter Sunday but, hearing of the plans at the last moment, and of the loss of the shipment of arms, the Chief of Staff of the Volunteers, Eoin MacNeill, intervened to stop what he feared would be a massacre. The Sunday papers had carried an order by MacNeill cancelling the Easter manoeuvres. Convinced that they faced imminent arrest, the revolutionaries decided to strike on the following day.

Because of the confusion caused by MacNeill's countermanding order, what had been intended as a co-ordinated surprise attack lost all semblance of order. Men heard by chance that they were wanted. Some chose to continue with their bank holiday plans; others reported without uniform or arms. Many could not find their units. Michael Boland, for example, had got an order to mobilise his local battalion at 9.30 that morning. After a great deal of to-ing and fro-ing they arrived at the city at about 12.30. As he wrote in his report:

> I tuch [sic] the 39 men under me into Liberty Hall which was held by a cupple of the C.A. I tuck it over awaiting orders. I despacth a note to Chief Command P.H. Pierce stating where I was and the number of men under me after some time I got a despatch to get all over to G.P.O. ... I succeeded in getting into Princes St when the cavalry maid their 1st charge on G.P.O. but were driven back with rifle fire from the north side of the G.P.O. during that attack. I had my men ready to meet them in Princes St but owing to them being beaten back it didn't come our turn to open fire on them.

A number of events crop up in almost all accounts of the GPO action, and the cavalry charge is one of them. Shortly after one o'clock a group of lancers rode down O'Connell Street from the Rotunda Hospital, sent to investigate rumours of the activity at the GPO. In later reconstructions they tend to be represented as cantering down the street with swords aloft, like a misplaced scene from the Crimea. Despite Connolly's efforts to keep the men from firing before the body of lancers drew level with the GPO, some guns were discharged early. The majority of the horsemen wheeled round and galloped back up O'Connell Street, but three men were killed. Several Volunteer statements record how a young lad ran up to one of the wounded men and grabbed his rifle, which he thrust through a window of the GPO.

Along with the charge on the GPO, and the reading of the Proclamation, both of which were witnessed by relatively few people, and understood by even fewer, the attack on the lancers has achieved iconic status in the story of the Rising. There are several reasons for this. Not only did the shooting take place in the middle of the street, and was therefore seen by rebels in the GPO and surrounding buildings, and by passers-by, but one of the horses lay by the Pillar all week as a reminder. Eyewitnesses repeatedly commented on the rotting carcass. Then there was the excitement of those rebels who couldn't hold their fire. While the shooting of the lancers was used as evidence of callousness by the British, for the rebel story it emphasised commitment and enthusiasm. Undoubtedly it was remembered as a turning point by the rebels: their first real engagement with British forces. But it was also the first of many clashes during the week between modernity and the old order. Like a terrifically speeded-up version of the First World War, the battle in Dublin was to span a whole array of battle strategies, from cavalry charge to bombardment and shelling in a few days.

That day and the next, despite gleeful looting of local shops by Dublin's poorer citizens, and isolated shooting incidents, the atmosphere remained mostly calm. But although the rebels were bunkering down for a siege (while they waited

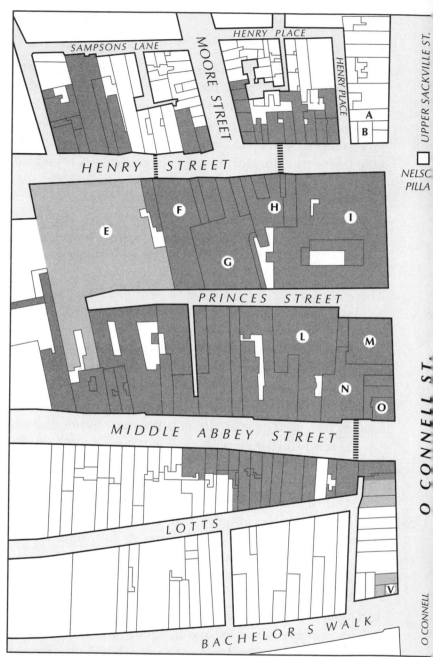

5. Based on a map issued by the Hibernian Fire and General Insurance Company shortly after the Rising, this plan also shows the principle barricades built by the insurgents during the week.

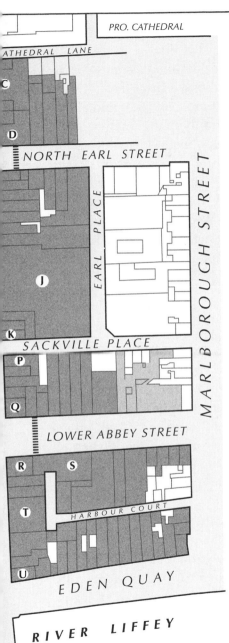

A PLAN OF THE GPO AREA

■ Destroyed buildings

■ Partially destroyed buildings

□ Uninjured buildings

IIIIIIII Barricades

A Nobletts s
B The Arch
C Lawrence s toy shop
D Tyler s Boots
E Arnott & Co. Ltd. Drapers
F Bewley Sons & Co.
G Coliseum Variety Theatre
H MacInerney & Co. Drapers
I *General Post Office*
J Clery & Co. and Imperial Hotel
K True Form Boot Co.
L Freeman s Journal
M Hotel Metropole
N Eason & Son Ltd. Newsagents
O Mansfield Boot-Makers
P Hoyte & Son
Q Hibernian Bank
R Reis and Co.
S Wynne s Hotel
T D. B. C. Restaurant
U Hopkins & Hopkins
V Kelly s Fort

for the rest of the country to rise) the slow response of the Crown authorities, and the layout of the city – the GPO was right next to a large slum district of small lanes and alleys, and crumbling tenements – meant there was nothing static about these first days of the Republic. As Volunteers got their orders, or heard the news through rumour and gossip, they began making their way into the city. Dribs and drabs of insurgents, and the women of Cumann na mBan, were still coming in to the GPO until Wednesday. A group from Kildare walked through Monday night to arrive on Tuesday morning. (Clarke promptly sent out a young woman to find them socks: 'A plentiful supply was given me by Mrs Joe McGuinness.') Relatives arrived at the GPO bringing tea and sandwiches, or to call their sons and daughters home. One rebel, a journalist called Knightly who was posted on the ground floor of the building, recalled handing a shilling to a passer-by out of a ground-floor window and asking for a stop press (which was brought back to him). While some volunteers 'melted away', as one stalwart put it, after the first few hours on Monday, the general excitement kept others going. A female volunteer who worked in the kitchen all week went home on Monday night but returned on Tuesday with her aunt: 'It was a lovely week and we did not feel the time flying.'

In the weeks and months after the executions of the most prominent rebels, most of the tales told of the events that week centred on the lost leaders. It may be for this reason that the story of what happened in the GPO can seem oddly static, concentrating reverentially on remembered tableaux, such as the spiritual Pearse heartening the men with rousing oratory, or the brave Connolly lying with his ankle shattered on his bed on wheels (and reading detective fiction).

The stories of the rank and file in the GPO are both more commonplace and more typical: stories of boredom, fear, exhaustion, hunger, but also excitement, risk, even flirtation. They are also stories that evoke a very familiar and local landscape. Participant accounts are often hazy on exactly what time an event occurred, but never on exactly where. Post-Rising Dublin saw the development of a kind of official rebellion topography of the O'Connell Street area – in which the GPO rose like a fortress from an otherwise flat landscape, a few other significant buildings (hotels mostly) doing their best to keep the great building company. But individual accounts of the Rising offer a very different sense of the local landscape. The GPO lay at the centre of a network of small streets, alleys, lanes and passages. Much of the activity in the GPO depended on the rebels' in-depth knowledge of this area – many of them lived in shouting distance of the building or had friends and relatives there. This streetscape was augmented by a parallel 'insurgent' network connecting up buildings by boring through internal walls, laying planks between rooftops, and setting up barricades between streets and alleys. But it was also a network of people – local inhabitants whose attitudes towards the Rising ranged from disapproval, to active support (carrying arms, providing food, delivering messages), to more neutral sympathy, like the group of men one insurgent stumbled across midweek, still drinking in a pub in Abbey Street, who told him to beware of 'them milithary in Capel Street'.

This contrast between public event and private experience is marked in nearly all the stories of that week. In the same way, 'official' accounts tended to tell the story as an event in military history, using the language of company and battalion, of rank, duty and command. The point was to present the Army of the Republic as a legitimate army, engaged in fighting as valid as the fighting in France or Flanders. Individual participant accounts, by contrast, rarely referred to people by rank, company or battalion. Orders came from individuals; tasks were done by or for friends. This informality is a feature of many war reminiscences – it is marked in First World War trench stories, for example. But it also offers an insight into the rebels' difficulties in measuring up to a 'proper' army.

The newly styled Army of the Republic was comprised of Irish Volunteers, men of the Irish Citizen Army, the women of Cumann na mBan and a few enthusiastic civilians (including some British, a few Swedish, and at least one Spaniard who fought in the GPO). The army laboured under a number of disadvantages: lack of men, uniforms, arms and ammunition. Patrick Colgan had returned to Ireland from Britain at the beginning of 1916, to avoid conscription. He had joined the camp at the Plunketts' house at Kimmage, which by the spring was employed full time in making improvised grenades, filling cartridges with buckshot, and making crude bayonets and home-made bombs. On Easter Monday morning he had travelled into town with sixty others, on two trams. 'Our arms consisted of a shot-gun and pike to each man. Pikes, incidentally, were also made at Kimmage. I think it was 100 rounds of shotgun ammunition we were given, and a certain number of us had revolvers.' If the pikes harked back to 1798, and the shotguns to farming, the insurgents were also no strangers to European revolutionary discourse, and the language of urban warfare:

When we marched into O'Connell Street our section commander, Joe Gahan, shouted, 'Military coming; man the barricades'. Why he shouted this direction I cannot say as, in fact, there were no barricades erected at the time. I think what he meant was to put up barricades.

Barricades were a practical and necessary part of street fighting, but they were also an echo of the battles for the French republic, one of several 'models' at work in conceptions of the Rising. As Colgan went on to explain, however, it initially proved hard to get people behind this popular uprising:

> We did not in fact erect barricades in O'Connell Street. The section Commander led us to Mooney's public house in Abbey Street which we tried to occupy but the manager had banged the hall door against us and we could not get entrance to the upper part of it. Martin Gleeson, who was with us, fired a shot at the lock but it failed to make any impression and then we moved a couple of doors further down Abbey Street and occupied the Ship Hotel. We got to work immediately in barricading the windows.

This haphazard, ad hoc response to the situation was the norm, prompting the question, what would have happened had the Rising gone off as planned on the Sunday? How would the rebels have got into the GPO with the doors banged against them?

When the main body of men charged the Post Office, Liam Daly was ordered to create a barricade on Lower Abbey Street. He used a combination of furniture, paper rolls from a newspaper store and bicycles. Detachments of men were sent to cover the approaches over O'Connell Bridge, Henry Street and Abbey Street, and to set up posts in the Hibernian Bank and the Imperial Hotel. In Hopkins and Hopkins, a jeweller's on the corner of Eden Quay, Charlie Turner found they had only glass cases for barricades. Their instructions were to break through the walls to link with another detachment in Reis's, a jeweller's and wireless repair outfit on the corner of Abbey Street. Turner had no tools, so he returned to the GPO for equipment and men. Later that day he went back again for supplies of food, munitions and bombs. It took them until Wednesday to break through the walls to Reis's. Meanwhile the men at the Wireless School at Reis's were attempting to assemble the disconnected wireless apparatus (an old 1.5 kw ship's transmitter) and erect an aerial on the roof. (As Fergus O'Kelly put it, 'The latter was rendered difficult by enemy snipers'.) Another group occupied Kelly's, a fishing tackle and gunpowder shop at the corner of O'Connell Street and Bachelor's Walk, and still another took over the Tower Bar on Henry Street. Here, too, they had difficulty in persuading the public of the seriousness of the enterprise:

> We later had to disperse looters who broke in while we were upstairs and took temporary charge of shop and dished out drink to all and sundry. However, we soon cleared these out and boarded up windows etc. We then took possession of the Arch licensed premises, Marks jewellers, Lairds, Nobletts and broke our way through latter premises into Royal Bank of Ireland and other premises.

Inside the GPO the barricading continued, and on Connolly's instructions a phone line was set up from the ground floor to the roof. It was on the roof that the men were to have the hottest time of it. Theirs was the most coveted post – it involved handling a gun rather than lugging material about to build barricades, or making loopholes and boring through walls – and it offered a great vantage point to pick out snipers and shoot at advancing infantry. Or so it appeared. For the rooftop men themselves it wasn't quite so rosy. For a start the parapet offered very little protection. It was about eighteen inches high, so the men had to lie prone or crouch in a space three or four feet wide between the parapet and the sloping roof behind them. British snipers on the roofs of the Gresham, Wynne's Hotel, the Carlisle Buildings, the Rotunda and Amiens Street station had a clear view of anyone who moved. There were a couple of trapdoors that led on to the roof, but Michael Boland – who spent most of the week up there – made a third by tearing off slates above the instrument room to make it easier to move around without coming under fire, and for lowering the wounded.

Nonetheless, by all accounts, once up on the roof you stayed up. The first contingent to be posted there on Monday stayed, eating and sleeping on the roof, until Wednesday. After a brief spell on the ground floor they were up again until Friday. Austin Kennan arrived in Dublin from London on Easter Sunday morning. He got to the GPO soon after it was occupied and was posted on the roof with another Londoner, Michael Mulvihill (who was killed in the evacuation of the building), and a Volunteer called Nugent. These three formed one of the many small groups on the roof, armed with shotguns and 'a quantity of bombs' (they used coats to cover them when it rained). They were fired on initially by rifles, later by machine guns and finally by artillery and incendiary shells. On Tuesday Pearse and Plunkett came up on the roof and Pearse 'spoke some encouraging words to us as he passed.' With the bombardment of the Citizen Army headquarters at Liberty Hall, Connolly paid a visit: 'the gist of what he said was "that the British were in a hurry to finish us, as they feared that reinforcements were coming to help us".' They were visited by a priest who climbed out to give them all 'conditional' absolutions. But that was about it. Most of the roofers tell stories of feeling forgotten, particularly in relation to food. 'They never sent as much as a biscuit up.'

Meanwhile some men remained at Liberty Hall through most of Monday. Later that afternoon Sean T. O'Kelly was again sent back there with a message for the officer in charge 'to wind up his job of bomb-making and come with his companions and all his bombs and other material to the Post Office'.

> One man had a tin or canister like a cocoa tin – there were hundreds of these in the room, some already filled, and some waiting to be filled. One would take a tin and put certain scraps of iron and other metal into it, it was handed to another man who put a different variety of metal into it, a third man had something else to put into it, and eventually one of them put in a little wire through a whole [sic] in the tin, and somebody else fitted percussion caps. Somebody else was stacking the finished tins in a corner.

This was evidently the first that O'Kelly had seen of bomb-making, but it had been going on for months in the Volunteer camps in the Dublin suburbs of Kimmage and Clontarf. All this ammunition now had to be shifted, along with the medical kits and supplies that the women of

Cumann na mBan had been preparing for weeks. The men began 'seizing all classes of vehicles for the transportation of our Arms and Ammunition to the post Office and also seizing various types of foodstuff which came along the Quays'. Joseph Cripps, a chemist who was in and out of the GPO all week, recalled:

> On Monday evening I was off duty and walked in a circle around the Post Office. Outside Liberty Hall, cabs proceeding with fares to the G.N. Railway were halted and the fares requested to walk. The cabs were utilized to remove supplies consisting of munitions to bedding.

Bread was commandeered from bakers' shops and milk from dairies. Food and bedding was brought from the Hotel Metropole, from the Imperial and from Clerys the department store. One man volunteered to secure a load of milk churns from the Dairy Engineering Co. stores. These were to be used for storing water in the GPO. He presciently 'also brought a large number of slash hooks for use in case our position was stormed'. He was off again then 'to commandeer buckets and whitewash brushes and superintend a staff of men posting through the city copies of the Proclamation'. Others used pages of Post Office stamps to stick the Proclamation up on walls and doors. (Sean T. O'Kelly had the presence of mind to post a copy as a keepsake to his mother – wisely he put the letter in a postbox some distance from the GPO.) This wasn't the only bit of fly-posting going on. The theatre critic Joseph Holloway recorded in his diary that the director of the Abbey theatre, St John Ervine, was in a terribly nervous state about the turn of events. Yeats's revolutionary play *Cathleen ni Houlihan* was

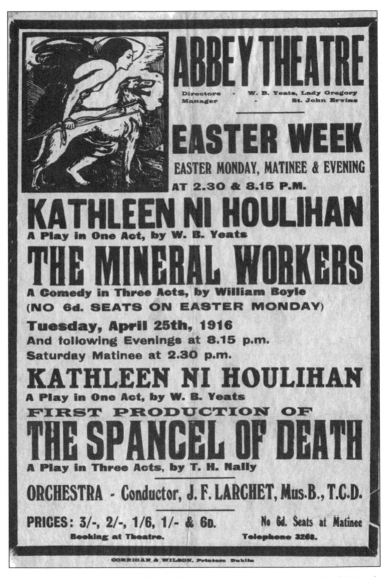

6. *A poster advertising the Abbey Theatre programme for Easter Week. Yeats's revolutionary play (the title misspelled with a 'K') was due to be performed twice on Easter Monday, before other revolutionary events took over.*

to be performed that night 'and might incite' the people. He quickly ran up a notice announcing the cancellation of the performance.

On his way back to the Post Office with a handcart of grenades, O'Kelly met Min Ryan, a member of Cumann na mBan who had spent the previous week carrying messages to Enniscorthy and Wexford. She had arrived back in Dublin on Sunday night, bringing her sister Phyllis with her, and on Monday morning she had reported to an address near Broadstone station. There she had spent the day sending girls out with messages to say their men were OK. At around 6 pm she was told she could go home:

> I remember a certain feeling of pleasure. I said: 'Now we can go around and see what is happening'. I remember Effie Taaffe and myself marched off with ourselves down-town, straight down along from Dorset St, to O'Connell St. We came openly down the street. There was an awful crowd of people gathered round in groups, watching. You could not get them to move off.

The distinction between the milling crowds and the rebels had yet to harden. Min Ryan and Joseph Cripps were not the only ones in the crowd in 'off-duty' mode – itself perhaps an odd concept for a revolution. The rebels were as keen as anyone else to see what was happening, and participants mixed with shoppers, travellers and local inhabitants. As Dubliners came back from their bank holiday jaunts in the early evening, the crowds swelled. Knots of people gathered at street corners to discuss the new situation, and the curious wandered from group to group trying to gather information. There were also some interested parties among the crowds.

At four o'clock in the afternoon Mrs Hamilton Norway, the wife of the Secretary of the Post Office, walked up O'Connell Street with her son to have a look: 'At every window were two men with rifles, and on the roof the parapet was lined with men. H's room appeared not to have been touched, and there were no men at his windows.' The theatre critic Joseph Holloway found himself sightseeing with the playwright T. H. Nally, whose play *The Spancel of Death* had also been cancelled by St John Ervine.

> All was quiet and we walked as far as O'Connell Bridge and then Nally said he'd like to see the Proclamation and I took him on to read it. Quite a number were doing the same.

What was the mood of this crowd? As Ryan suggests, the audience that gathered for the Rising was somewhat intractable – its demeanour curious rather than awed, or inspired. The novelist James Stephens, who wrote one of the first published accounts of the Rising, found some in the crowd, particularly women, fiercely critical of the Volunteers, but for the most part people were reticent about whether they were for or against them. 'Men met and talked volubly, but they said nothing that indicated a personal desire or belief.' News was eagerly exchanged but not opinions.

The principal puzzle was over what was going to happen. The Rising had taken everyone by surprise, including many of the Volunteers themselves, who had reported for manoeuvres, not open warfare. While the British authorities were watching events carefully in Ireland, no one seems to have anticipated imminent armed conflict. The Chief Secretary, Augustine Birrell, was in London. So too was

General Friend, who was in charge of the British troops in Ireland. Many of the British officers and men were at the race meeting at Fairyhouse on Easter Monday, and Dublin Castle in particular was virtually undefended. After three policemen were killed in the first hours of the rebellion, the Dublin Metropolitan Police Force was withdrawn from the streets. By late afternoon the Crown forces had begun to muster, and had made headway against rebel posts at the South Dublin Union and at City Hall, but for this first day – particularly at GPO Headquarters – the rebels appeared to have the advantage.

Yet although they had control of the telegraph room at the GPO, and had cut wires across the city, they had failed to seize the telephone exchange at Crown Alley. When the engineers at the Post Office were ejected by the rebels, several of them ran to Amiens Street station, where there was a small telegraph office. News of the Rising was telegraphed to London. Telephone calls were put through to the Naval Centre at Kingstown (Dun Laoghaire), which telegraphed the Admiralty and the War Office. Reinforcements for the British troops in Dublin were called in from the Curragh, and they began to arrive on Monday evening. Over Monday night, artillery was brought in from Athlone. On Tuesday, troops arrived from Belfast. Early on Wednesday morning, reinforcements would arrive from England. The forces were gathering for the counter-attack.

⊠

A persistent theme in almost all the participant accounts is the difficulty of being sure exactly when anything happened. As the week progressed and rebels became increasingly trapped inside the buildings, days merged into one another. It is partly for this reason that accounts of the Rising revert to 'shared' or well-known moments as a way of punctuating the week. The reading of the Proclamation; the hoisting of flags; the attack on the lancers; Pearse's tabletop speech to the men; Connolly's injury: all offered temporal bearings. Possibly the earliest participant account to attempt a day-by-day record of the events in the GPO was one written on a small scrap of paper and smuggled out of Stafford Detention Barracks. A similar diary was written on toilet paper in Wakefield prison. But newspaper accounts (particularly those published in Britain) had already attempted to capture the unfolding drama for their readers. The value put on journalistic immediacy reached its apogee in the 1966 television dramatisation of the Rising, which not only broadcast the events day by day over Easter week, but was staged as a drama documentary – with a reporter inside the GPO commenting on the events as they happened. Yet for all the obsession with the precise timing of incidents, there is no agreement on something as basic as how long the rebellion lasted. Diaries and memoirs put it at six days, seven days, even eight. No doubt the rebels' millenarian ambitions (proclaiming the First, then the Second Day of the Republic, and so on) increased this tendency. As Desmond FitzGerald wryly pointed out, this only seemed to be tempting fate, confirming that the Rising's days were numbered.

The insurgents' impulse to record their deeds ranged from the most practical of communications to the most lofty. Winny Carney, Connolly's secretary, had brought her typewriter with her. She spent the time typing out orders and instructions for the men in the various outposts. On Tuesday 25th, for example, she typed the following communiqué 'To

Officer in Charge' of Reis's and the D.B.C., the latter a restaurant owned by the Dublin Bread Company, just across
O'Connell Street:

> The main purpose of your post is to protect our wire-
> less station. Its secondary purpose is to observe Lower
> Abbey Street and Lower O'Connell Street. Commandeer
> in the D.B.C. whatever food and utensils you require.
> Make sure of a plentiful supply of water wherever you
> are. Break all glass in the windows of the rooms occu-
> pied by you for fighting purposes. Establish a connec-
> tion between your forces in the D.B.C. and in the Reis's
> building. Be sure that the stairways leading immediately
> to your rooms are well barricaded. We have a post in
> the house at the corner Bachelor's WALK, in the Hotel
> Metropole, in the Imperial Hotel, in General Post Office.
> The directions from which you are likely to be attacked
> are from the Customs House or from the far side of the
> river, Dolier Street or Westmoreland Street. We believe
> there is a sniper in McBurneys [*sic*] on the far side of the
> river.

> James Connolly
> Commandant General

Notes like this clattered from her typewriter, and young
women (and a few young men) were sent out with them
hidden under their hats, or sewn into the hems of their
clothing. They had instructions to eat them if they were
stopped. At the other end of the spectrum there were the
bulletins of *Irish War News*, written out by Pearse in copying
ink pencil on heavy typewriting paper – regular GPO stock

– and printed by O'Keefe, a jobbing printer with premises in Halston Street. The first issue appeared early Tuesday morning and the last – handwritten – on Friday.

Because of this urge to chronicle we have a great deal of hour-by-hour information on what was happening. At 4 am on Tuesday, for example, Connolly sent a man by bike to mobilise Enniscorthy: 'Cut the Railway line, and don't allow any troops through by train.' At 6 am Martin Lynch left the GPO and 'proceeded to Kennedy's Bakery, Great Britain St and secured delivery of 4 or 5 vanloads of bread for garrison'. He paid in cash for the order. He was then granted two hours' leave to return home for his uniform and equipment, and for the rest of the day he was placed on window duty. At 7 am the crowd from Kildare turned up. An hour later James Ryan, future Fianna Fáil minister, arrived. He had spent Monday trying to get back from Cork, where he had delivered MacNeill's countermanding order. When he got home he found his sisters waiting for him, to tell him to report to the GPO. As Min Ryan recalled:

> Phyllis is certain she brought his gun down for him under her long coat. The three of us walked the whole way to the G.P.O. along by Trinity College … I had a feeling there was something serious going on there. You would see an odd man peeping out from behind sandbags or you would see the muzzle of a gun.

She was right. From the Vice-Regal Lodge in Phoenix Park the Lord Lieutenant, Lord Wimborne, had been desperately calling for military reinforcements from England, though these men would not arrive until Wednesday. But the Officer's Training Corps at Trinity College had been reinforced during Monday night by men sent from the Curragh, under General Lowe, and they would soon be firing on the GPO. Meanwhile Wimborne had taken the dramatic step of declaring martial law.

But on Tuesday morning, with the police still off the streets and little sign of the army, the crowds around O'Connell Street were growing. Thomas King Moylan, a clerk in Grangegorman Mental Hospital and a playwright, wandered round the city after 8 am Mass. He found barricades around Stephen's Green, everything closed on Grafton Street and an entirely new regime ensconced at the GPO:

> I passed down Westmoreland street and over O'Connell Bridge, where I saw a squad of the Citizen Army (a labour organisation) with their guns and bayonets, bandoliers and haversacks, marching up Bachelor's Walk. O'Connell street was a very curious spectacle; all shops closed, the streets filled with wandering crowds of sightseers, and no vehicular traffic, except the ubiquitous bicycle. Across Abbey Street leading to the Custom House (of which the insurgents are stated to be in possession) was a barricade composed of crates of brand new bicycles taken out of Keating's shop, no one seemed to be in charge of it, but in the upper windows of Reis's shop were many volunteers, with desks and tables partially blocking up the window. At the opposite side of Abbey Street a beautiful shop front of Mansfield's, boot makers, was entirely gutted, being practically swept clear away. Lemon's sweet shop and Frewen's, a drapers, in O'Connell street, near Chancellor's, were also completely gutted. What a sight was the G.P.O. This building, which has recently been renovated,

had every window smashed to atoms and the openings stuffed with what appeared to be mail sacks. The glass from the broken windows was scattered wide into the middle of the street. What took place here I cannot say, but apparently the place was attacked in force from the street. A double line of barbed wire was stretched from the corner of the P.O. at Prince's street right across O'Connell street, and another double line from the Henry Street corner to the corner of Earl Street, North. At the bridge side of the wire was a Citizen Armyite, a low sized lad of about twenty or twenty-five in shabby clothes, bandolier and haversack, with a gun bearing a somewhat rusty looking bayonet, by his side. He was chatting with an onlooker, and apparently was only there for the purpose of seeing that the wire was not removed, as it was easy to pass under it, and no one was prevented from passing. Between the first wire and the pillar a dead horse lay on its side, amid a litter of glass, probably from the tram cars, of which a solitary one stood on the track leading to Earl Street. This street was also barricaded with shop counters, chairs, tables and shutters. The barricade was about eight feet high.

According to James Ryan the atmosphere around the GPO was one of 'exhilaration'. It was 'as if we had got rid of all alien authority'. Here the difference between the GPO and other rebel positions was at its most acute. Elsewhere the rebels were encamped inside buildings – some, like the group at Mount Street Bridge, were well placed to ambush enemy forces; others, like the men in Boland's Mill and Jacob's Biscuit Factory, were almost irrelevant to the fighting. At the GPO, by contrast, the entire area seemed for a time under the control of the Republic. And for the local inhabitants it appeared that all authority, alien or not, had gone by the board. They were quite happy to take advantage of the situation. Looting had begun on Monday night, but by Tuesday it was a severe problem for shopkeepers and insurgents alike. Shop owners and proprietors had no notion that the whole of O'Connell Street would be in flames by Friday. As it was they had to stand by as small groups led the way in looting. A priest staying at the Gresham Hotel on O'Connell Street explained, 'the way of it was you'd see a group of men and women coming along, and suddenly a man would take out a stone and smash a window, and then they'd all begin to smash and drag out handfuls of whatever it might be, jewellery or boots or toys or anything else.'

Many of the stories told by people unsympathetic to the looters – for the most part the extreme poor who lived in tenements close to the GPO – were tales of greed, of people trying to take so much they got nothing. The women who could not carry all the goods they had gathered up, the drunks who dressed up in finery and fought over it, the men taking luxuries they could not use. One rebel recalled that on Tuesday 'I took up post at the Henry Street-O'Connell Street corner and witnessed the deplorable looting that went on all morning and into the afternoon. I saw a man emerge from Lawrence's sports goods shop in Upper O'Connell Street, tee up golf balls and drive them down O'Connell Street. Women were trundling off hand-trucks of shoes, and I saw one woman with a piano on a truck.'

Others argued that it was initially hunger rather than plunder that drove people to looting, though here too it was the luxurious that drew people, as they gorged themselves on sweets and cakes they could never have tasted otherwise:

the 'sweet savour' of insurrection, as James Stephens put it. Either way, the notices that the pacifist Francis Sheehy Skeffington posted on O'Connell Bridge, calling for a force of citizens to stop the looting, were unlikely to have any effect. By mid morning Lawrence's was on fire, producing a whole new raft of dangers. Eamon Bulfin had been on the roof of the GPO since Monday lunchtime:

> I remember we were still on the roof when Lawrence's went on fire. It was a sports shop, and all the kids brought out a lot of fireworks, made a huge pile of them in the middle of O'Connell Street, and set fire to them … We had our bombs on top of the Post Office, and these fireworks were shooting up in the sky. We were very nervous. There were Catherine Wheels going up O'Connell Street and Catherine Wheels coming down O'Connell Street.

One Volunteer was detailed to take 'a squad of men to stop the looting, to keep the crowd out of the firemen's way and endeavour to prevent men and women jumping from the roof of the building on Sackville Place … I had to fire shots over heads of people.' It may be this incident that gave rise to rumours that the fire brigade was fired on 'by the Sinn Féiners', as reported by Mrs Hamilton Norway.

Drunken parties in the street, fireworks displays, groups of people chatting at the barricades and street corners and taking advantage of the fine weather: the carnival atmosphere was annoying to the Volunteers, as it suggested that this was not a serious rebellion. Several eyewitnesses noted that the looters respected an area in front of the GPO, between the two lines of barbed wire. Although dispatch riders and supply vans were going in and out under the wire, the looters kept clear. Nonetheless, the looting and raucousness meant that the rebellion seemed somehow unreal. Moreover, the looters' acknowledgement of the armed insurrection applied to only a rather small area, and as the day wore on even this element of respect diminished. Many of the barricades were stuffed with furniture, serviceable sofas and chairs, not to mention brand-new bicycles and rolls of cloth. As Diarmuid Lynch put it, 'During the night stronger steps had to be resorted to against the looting element in Henry Street who grabbed promiscuous articles from the barricades then in course of construction.'

While carnival reigned, the rebels continued to make fast their positions, in expectation of an infantry assault. Throughout the day they continued boring through internal walls to secure the shopfronts the length of O'Connell Street. By Tuesday lunchtime they had the run of the houses between Lower Abbey Street and Sackville Place. By Wednesday they had from the corner of Eden Quay right up to North Earl Street. The whole of Lower O'Connell Street on both sides could be negotiated inside buildings; barricades covered the street crossings. Connolly spent much of the day creating and reinforcing outposts in a circle around the GPO. Within the building the men settled down to sentry duties and continued with bomb-making – by this point they were filling cans and pipes with type from the offices of the *Freeman's Journal*.

By Tuesday the men at Reis's had managed to get the wireless transmitter working. A first communiqué was sent out stating that Republic was proclaimed and that Dublin City was in the hands of the Republican troops. This message was apparently picked up and relayed to the United States by ships at sea. A series of numbered communiqués were sent out in Morse code on Tuesday and Wednesday, but by Wednesday evening Reis's was on fire and the wireless contingent had to return to the GPO, bringing bits of apparatus with them on an upturned table.

Meanwhile, groups of insurgents were still making their way to the GPO. Towards evening on Tuesday another sixty-five men turned up from the north of the city. As Frank Henderson described it, they made their way against a tide of refugees: 'There was at this time a continuous stream of civilians in flight from the city, families with whatever belongings they could gather going to relatives who lived outside the city. Some indeed apparently did not know where they were going – some were terror-stricken – some merely anxious, and not a few wished us success and words of encouragement.' The Volunteers had picked up a number of khaki-clad British soldiers on the way, who they were holding as prisoners, and as they crossed O'Connell Street to enter the GPO the group were fired on by the men staking out the Imperial Hotel opposite. Connolly ran into the road with his hands above his head to stop the firing.

It was after the arrival of this large group that Pearse performed his most stirring piece of oratory, standing up on a table and 'pouring out his soul' to the men. Oscar Traynor recalled the gist of the speech, which may have been less difficult it seems because it echoed parts of Tuesday's war bulletin and anticipated parts of Wednesday's:

'We have wiped out the blackest stain in Irish history, the execution of Robert Emmet in the midst of a vast gathering of Irishmen who let him die without a single protest.' He further stated that, 'In the course of a few hours all

7. A drawing by Charles Saurin, of Pearse addressing the men from
Fairview, who arrived at the GPO on Tuesday: 'We have wiped out the
blackest stain in Dublin's history – that of 1803'. Pearse stands on a table
between the arched sandbagged windows of the public office.

would be fighting for our freedom in the streets of our
city and that victory would be ours, even though it might
be that victory would be found in death.'

Clearly this speech was inspiring. Months later one of
the insurgents held at the internment camp at Frongoch
in Wales, Charles Saurin, drew a sketch of the scene, even
though it transpires he was not even in the GPO at the time.
(The sketch may have been a way of making up for missing
this epic moment while he was having his thumb band-
aged.) Pearse's speech on Tuesday crops up again and again

in accounts of the week, though this may be partly because as far as the majority of men in the GPO were concerned it was one of the few moments they had direct contact with Pearse himself. Connolly raced around giving orders, setting up outposts and inspecting defences. Pearse seems to have sat silent for long periods, or engaged in quiet one-to-one conversations. Desmond Ryan, for example, recalled that on what he called the 'worst' night:

> when the fires glared in on the ground floor of the GPO, Pearse came and sat beside me. He was seated on a barrel, his slightly flushed face crowned by his turned-up military hat ... 'Well, *when* we are all *wiped out*, people will blame us for everything, condemn us, but only for this protest the war would have ended and nothing would have been done. After a few years they will see the meaning of what we tried to do.'

The imminent wipe-out appears to have been on everyone's mind. Min Ryan recalled that on Tuesday night (the same night as Pearse's speech) Tom Clarke spoke to her.' "I'd like to tell you a few things because ... we of course here will be completely wiped out." He said we here, meaning the Head and the people. "We'll all be wiped out," he said, "but you and some others may escape." ' He was 'quite gay' about it, and she described trying to keep a serene face as 'my brother was in there, in the wiping out you know.' According to Ryan, Clarke offered the following rationale for the Rising. Firstly, he argued, it was vital that a protest was made before the end of the war, so that the declaration of the Republic could come before the nations at the peace conference. And for the protest to carry any weight it had to be spectacular. Secondly, the Rising was intended to rouse the national spirit in the Irish people and to combat British propaganda. 'And the only way to do that is sacrifice.' And thirdly, he held that a volunteer army couldn't survive without something to do.

There seems to have been a bit of sibling rivalry over this conversation, as her brother James recalled that Clarke said all this to him, though it is quite possible Clarke was singling out lots of people as potential survivors of the wiping out. It is equally plausible that someone else passed down these justifications for the wipe-out. What is certain is that similar words and phrases were attributed to nearly all the leaders. Domhnall Ó Buachalla had arrived from Kildare that morning:

> We got into the Post Office. Every place was quiet at that period. Numbers of people were on the street looking around. We had tea and eggs and cigars. I thought we should have got a rest. Connolly paraded us and said, 'it didn't matter a damn if we were wiped out now as we had justified ourselves'. I thought it a bit rugged.

Desmond FitzGerald went further and attributed the phrase to himself. On his first sight of the flag flying above the GPO he apparently turned to his wife and said, 'This is worth being wiped out for.' His memoir (written in the 1940s) repeats the phrase three times.

It is not hard to see why in this period of lull before the battle proper, the enormity of what they had taken on, and the impossibility of going back, bore in on the leaders. While the rank and file of the Volunteer forces were kept busy boring holes or making bombs, the leaders worried over the moral and theological justifications for their actions – though the collective kneeling for the rosary, the confessions, the discussion of whether the Pope had sent his blessing were all ways in which the 'ordinary' insurgents could address the moral probity of the rebellion. Nonetheless, given the few recollections of conversations (rather than actions) in the GPO, the recurrence of the 'wipe-out' is striking. It was a phrase that could convey both justification and outcome in one phrase. Indeed, it allowed a slippage from one to the other. When Pearse claimed that the blackest stain in Irish history had been washed away, he was recalling the Christian language of sacrifice, the idea that Christ's blood on the cross had wiped away the stain of sin from the world. As Oscar Wilde put it in characteristically mordant terms in 'The Ballad of Reading Gaol', 'And only blood can wipe out blood'.

A place at the peace table was not to be gained by merely symbolic actions, however. The rebels isolated in the GPO increasingly had to face the fact that wiping out the stain of history was only going to occur by being wiped out themselves. This meaning of the term – utter destruction by the enemy – was a relatively new one in 1916. It had become popular in late Victorian boys' adventures, such as the best-selling novels and stories of H. Rider Haggard and Rudyard Kipling. It is a favourite phrase in the imperial adventure fantasies of G. A. Henty, for example, which in turn fed into the rhetoric of courage and noble sacrifice in the trenches. The phrase blended hopelessness with courage and Christian virtue, and was one of the many moments when the battle in Dublin echoed the larger war on the continent. It was also perhaps the first moment that the 'sacrificial' nature of the undertaking was openly acknowledged. There was a growing awareness that it was not going to be easy to get out of this. The wipe-out was a way of addressing the coming rout and making it seem glorious – wiping out the blackest stain. But so far from a general willing embrace of sacrifice, there were clearly many people who thought the idea 'a bit rugged'.

2

DESTRUCTION

The extra-ordinary thing to us is that there seems to be such a lull all over the place. The day is a close, sultry affair, inclined to rain and as if thunder were in the air. The rattle of a cart along the streets seems now like marching men and then like the rattle of a machine gun. Isolated reports are heard on and off, but the fighting, if there is to be any fighting has not yet started, although this trouble broke out about noon yesterday, nor does there seem to be any move towards fighting. The Volunteers and the Citizen Army are at their barricades and in the houses round the City while the soldiers are locked up and seemingly making no move to attack. How, when, where the first contest will start we have not the vaguest notion, and certainly never was an attempt made to inaugurate a republic in such a peculiar fashion as at the present. We are full of surmises, wondering what the Republicans are aiming at, wondering what the military will do, getting no news from anywhere outside and wondering what is happening in other parts; if England has been isolated telegraphically and whether the warships will arrive with reinforcements; if this has been planned in conjunction with a raid on England by the Germans and in fact any sane or insane possibility is trotted out, inspected,

discussed and relegated to the region where go those things
that time alone can tell.

Thomas King Moylan's diary, Tuesday 25 April 1916

Fittingly for a building whose purpose was communication, the GPO started producing text almost as soon as it was occupied. There were official communiqués from both sides: bulletins, memoranda, manifestos, messages telegraphed to the world from O'Connell Street; and from the civil authorities announcements of curfews, proclamations of martial law and soon afterwards the reports of the Commissions of Inquiry. There were the personal stories by observers and participants, the day-by-day diaries written by onlookers caught up in the events, the letters home to England by 'loyalists' horrified by the violence, rebel accounts written in prison, reports by post-office employees. Much of this material was published almost immediately after the surrender. Books such as the novelist James Stephens's account, *The Insurrection in Dublin*, and articles in all the major British and Irish journals and papers dissected the event from every conceivable political stance. These publications catered for the voyeurism of the British public, but also for Dubliners' almost insatiable need to understand what they had been through.

The Rising is a rare treat in the history of political insurrection before the age of television, an event that was anatomised at the time from dozens of perspectives. This is partly because it occurred less than 300 miles from the metropolis: a colonial-style conflict had erupted in the Empire's backyard, and news was able to travel fast. The moment there was a let-up in the security situation the London newspapers dispatched reporters; within a few days of the surrender the

8. One of the questionnaires designed by Diarmuid Lynch in the mid 1930s, the basis for what he hoped would be the official history of the GPO area. Respondents were asked to detail their posts, superior officers, and their duties throughout the week.

newsreels were coming in. But it was also because the insurgency's leaders were well-educated, highly literate men who knew the value of communication. Likewise Dublin was full of well-educated citizens whose natural response was to write about what they had witnessed. This extraordinary level of documentation has bequeathed a multidimensional image of armed rebellion, enabling us to share the standpoint of the combatants, of the curious onlooker, of the shopper caught up in the events, of those listening out for every breath of rumour. Like contemporary mass media coverage, the documentation of the Rising offers a mixture of heroics, self-interest, voyeurism and the strange obstinacy of everyday life, even in the midst of violence and turmoil.

Yet despite, or because of, the mountains of first-hand testimony, there was little agreement over what had happened. The reams of ephemeral documents produced further records, as the first layer of analysis was augmented and overlaid in response to a voracious appetite for more information, particularly on the rebel side. In some cases rival accounts were politically motivated – members of the pro-treaty civil war faction praised the role of Michael Collins (who was aide-de-camp to Joseph Plunkett), for example. Memoirs, histories, exhaustive questionnaires sent to veterans of the rebellion: all form the raw material for our picture of what was happening inside and outside the GPO.

We know, for example – in extraordinary detail – exactly what happened to those rebels who were privileged enough to hear the wipe-out speech on Tuesday. Pumped full of Pearsian oratory the new arrivals were brought out into O'Connell Street where Connolly divided them into three groups, detailed to create a new outpost in the Hotel Metropole and to fortify the positions in the Imperial Hotel and in Henry Street. This last group was ordered to put up barricades either side of Moore Street:

> We had to construct these of whatever materials came to our hands. One of them was partly composed of bales of cloth taken from a tailors shop, but the mob which was now in the street ran away with the bales as quickly as our men put them down. To stop this I ordered shots to be fired over their heads but they paid no attention to this. Finally I ordered a bayonet charge and this had the desired result.

This group was also in charge of boring holes through internal walls from the back of the GPO through to Bewley's, the Coliseum Theatre and then on to Arnotts, the department store. For all the trouble with looters the men did attract some support: 'A milkman brought us milk two or three times during the day and came again on Thursday. He refused to accept payment and was most enthusiastic in his wishes for our success.'

We know rather less about how ordinary citizens were faring across the city, but the literary diarists help fill in the picture. By Thursday the rebels boring along Henry Street were almost the only people in the city to have a ready supply of milk. For ordinary residents it was almost as difficult to get milk and bread as it was to get news. St John Ervine was embarrassed to recall that on the Tuesday the residents of his club on Stephen's Green had lamented the lack of milk for breakfast, even while a dead man still lay on the pavement outside. By the end of the week James Stephens was beginning his diary each day with a list of basic foodstuffs which had run out. No food had been brought into the city since Saturday.

Despite the lucky few supplied with milk, the question of food loomed large inside the GPO all week. It was, to say the least, unevenly distributed. Men on the roof complained they were left without so much as a biscuit. Even on the second floor, insurgents recalled they were left without food from Tuesday to Thursday, when Desmond FitzGerald arrived with 'a bucket of tea'. On the other hand, those who made it to the dining room were served lavish and almost formal dinners. As FitzGerald recalled, some of the men had little to do for long stretches at a time, and made themselves more than comfortable at the dinner tables, while others were not relieved at their posts and went hungry.

Louise Gavan Duffy (who was then a teacher at St Mary's University College, Dublin) had turned up at the GPO on Monday afternoon. Because of her broadly pacifist principles she refused to do 'active' work – such as carrying messages – but she was happy to work in the kitchen. She stayed there all week, occasionally snatching some sleep on a mattress in one of the corridors. In the first days, as food was brought in from the Imperial and the Metropole hotels, and from the provision stores in Henry Street, those in charge of the kitchen were asked to calculate how long the provisions would last. They reckoned they had enough for a three-week fight. This didn't include supplying food to other positions in the city, but through Tuesday and Wednesday it became clear that some posts were without any sort of provisions at all. Fifteen-year-old Mary McLoughlin spent much of Tuesday dragging sackfuls of food from the GPO to the College of Surgeons, helped by Hanna Sheehy Skeffington. Her brother Sean meanwhile was taking parcels of food to the Mendicity Institute. On the Tuesday morning Dick Humphreys was detailed to take the O'Rahilly's De Dion car, with a long list of requirements from FitzGerald, and to commandeer what he could. As he put it, 'we become expert house-breakers', loading the car to such an extent that he feared for the axle.

But the principal task in the kitchen was cooking and dishing up food to the 400 or so men in the GPO. All the paraphernalia of plates and cutlery produced mountains of washing up:

> There were a couple of prisoners there. One was a British officer, who just sat there looking glum. He was not asked to do any work, but the Tommies were washing up. There were two or three Tommies who were quite cheerful. I think they were in uniform. They were taken prisoners in the street.

Several of the rebels mention the miserable British officer in their accounts, including some rather dismissive comments about his drinking, and his abject fear under the bombardment towards the end of the week. From our contemporary perspective it is clear he was suffering from shell shock. At any rate, he was in no fit state to help with the cooking but the Tommies were aided by a small army of women. When Phyllis Ryan arrived with her brother on Tuesday morning she was put under Gavan Duffy.

> I was put to carve a lot of beef. At that time there were nearby the Metropole, the DBC and the Imperial Hotel. All the stuff that was in these places was commandeered and brought into the Post Office and receipts were given on behalf of the Irish Republican Army. I remember carving, carving.

For all the industrial canteen numbers, however, Fitz-Gerald seems to have been keen to run his dining room on surprisingly formal lines. When two young women were promoted to officers 'on the field' for particular distinction in dispatch carrying, they were permitted to eat at a separate table in the dining room. ('We thought it was marvellous.') The ceremony of officers' tables was only one example of the care lavished on dining. FitzGerald had been part of pre-war avant-garde literary circles in London – friends with T. E. Hulme, H. D., Harold Munro and Richard Aldington – and he was used to a decent class of dinner. He may also have felt the rather fancy hotel fare that had been commandeered deserved generous treatment. At any rate Mary McLaughlin recalled that when she was brought up to the kitchen, exhausted after a day of back and forth to the College of Surgeons, 'This was the first time I saw a whole salmon cooked laid on a dish.'

Diarists and letter-writers who recorded the events in the city as they unfolded were partly responding to the absence of information from official sources. They had little knowledge about what was happening, and even less about how things would turn out. It was late on the Tuesday night that Thomas King Moylan confided his 'sane and insane' speculations to his diary. News of the Rising in the Dublin-based papers was confined to a three-line announcement in the *Irish Times*, and no English or country papers were available. Into this vacuum rumours flooded: there were German submarines off the coast of Leinster, which had been landing machine guns, rifles and ammunition; thousands of insurgents were marching on Dublin – 3,000 had set off for the GPO from Belfast alone; Verdun had fallen to the Germans; Cork city had been taken by the rebels; Zeppelins were raiding London; the German fleet in the North Sea were endeavouring to land in England. Someone confided to St John Ervine that the Pope had committed suicide, and that Orangemen were marching on Dublin in support of the Sinn Féiners.

Some rumours turned out to be true, for example that transports of soldiers had been sent from England, and that the pacifist Francis Sheehy Skeffington had been arrested while attempting to stop the looting, and taken to Portobello Barracks, where he had been shot in cold blood, along with two other men. When soldiers arrived to search Sheehy Skeffington's home, his seven-year-old son watched his mother take from the mantelpiece a postcard from an academic friend in Germany and tear it into tiny pieces. Between them they ate it.

Despite the fact that the capital was quickly cut off – the Crown forces swiftly took control of the major train stations and of the roads leading into and out of the city – rumours travelled rapidly through the country as a whole. Katherine Tynan, a writer and friend of Yeats, was across the other side of the country in Mayo. There the first sign that anything had occurred came on Tuesday, when there were no letters. The first rumours were whispered on Tuesday afternoon and after that, as she said, they came 'thick and fast'. The principal fear was of a possible German invasion. 'One imagined the spiked helmets coming in a line above the tops of the hedgerows.'

Tynan was taking the temperature among her friends, of course, who were supporters of the Irish Parliamentary Party leader John Redmond and of the British war effort. Yet similar rumours raced through the GPO. As the rebels argued among themselves over the case for international recognition of the Republic, and a place at the peace conference, 'the rumours were rife that "the Germans were in Dublin Bay and on the Naas Road". Also that there had been a big fight in Limerick and that the Poet had sent his blessing.' Patrick Colgan, one of the Maynooth men, recalled his response to this news: 'I was thrilled to think the Germans had selected Kildare to land in. It never struck me Kildare being inland it wasn't possible at that time to land there.'

The Kildare coast was a stretch, but most of the rumours were not as insane as might now appear. Long before the line in the Proclamation about the 'gallant allies in Europe' became widely known, Sinn Féin propaganda had set up an expectation of German aid. Tynan's invading German helmets were a stock image in pro-war propaganda – stoking fears of teutonic raids; by contrast Arthur Griffith had argued that Ireland had 'nothing to fear from the Germans'. The Irish underground press had reprinted German arguments for Irish freedom from the British Empire, suggesting that a Germany victory would result in immediate independence. An issue of the radical underground paper *The Spark*, published in March 1916, had included an invasion fantasy story, in which the Germans arrive and Irish Volunteers co-ordinate a rising across the island and found a republic. Although Arthur Griffith's separatist political organisation Sinn Féin was not behind the Rising (it was not until 1917 that Arthur Griffith's Sinn Féin formally joined with republicans to form the new Sinn Féin party), it was no surprise that the majority of Dubliners assumed they were living through a Sinn Féin rebellion. Not only did much of the insurgents' rhetoric echo Sinn Féin's manifestos, but several prominent rebels were members of Sinn Féin as well as of the Volunteers.

But the real impetus behind rebel rumours of the impending arrival of the Germans was as a way of coping with the fear of imminent attack by the imperial forces – a way of fending off the wipe-out. For it was clear by Wednesday that the British were now in position and that the firing was hotting up. General Lowe had snipers on the roofs and inside many of the buildings around the GPO: the Rotunda, McBirneys, the Carlisle Buildings, the Model Schools, the Gresham, Wynne's hotel. The building was all but surrounded. There was a small force with machine guns at Amiens Street station, and two eighteen-pounder guns were now in position on the roof of Trinity College. In addition, early on Wednesday the gunboat *Helga* sailed up the Liffey and began pounding Liberty Hall. Martial law had been declared and anyone out on the streets was at risk.

Ironically it was on Wednesday that some eyewitnesses began to record a feeling among ordinary Dubliners that the Volunteers might be able to hold out. As James Stephens put it, 'There is almost a feeling of gratitude towards the Volunteers because they are holding out for a little while, for had they been beaten the first or second day the City would have been humiliated to the soul.' Such sentiments suggest that Pearse's claim to have redeemed Ireland's honour was not quite as outlandish as might now appear. At any rate he may have struck a chord among the silent onlookers. Stephens admitted that most people who were ready to risk an opinion on the Rising were 'definitely Anti-Volunteer'. But he found many more who were non-committal. Tellingly he described everyone he met as trying to read the 'secret' opinions of others. There was little to be gained by coming out in favour of the rebels and a great deal to be lost if, as seemed inevitable, they were beaten. But there was also the basic difficulty of taking the new situation in. As Stephens put it, 'None of these people were prepared for Insurrection. The thing has been sprung on them so suddenly that they were unable to take sides, and their feeling of detachment was still so complete that they would have betted on the business as if it had been a horse race or a dog fight.'

By Wednesday morning these street-corner conversations were only happening at a good distance from the GPO. The streets in the centre of the city were now very dangerous. In addition to the tremendous noise of the shells firing from the *Helga*, there were machine guns, shotguns, rifle fire (several observers spent time trying to distinguish the sound of the British Lee-Enfield from the antiquated 'Howth Mausers' used by the rebels). While soldiers with experience of the Western Front argued that the shelling was not nearly so bad in Dublin, there was general agreement that the machine gun and rifle fire was worse. For a start it was impossible to tell, in the narrow streets and ragged rooftops, where it was coming from. Rebels posted to the windows and on the roofs devoted a great deal of time in their statements to pinpointing the exact locations of enemy snipers, giving a sense of their preoccupations.

As far as possible the rebels moved around through the buildings, and under shelter of the barricades. They rigged up a cord between the Imperial and the GPO, so that they could send messages across in a can. They used semaphore. And they kept the quick dashes across the street under fire to a minimum. But it was still necessary to make some journeys further afield. A contingent of volunteers continued to make bombs (the large piles of explosive cans would prove a problem when the fires began in the GPO). By now they were filling the cans with type from the *Freeman's Journal* offices across Prince's Street, but they had run out of fuses and detonators. At 6 am on Wednesday Joseph Cripps made a dash for supplies to a chemist in Bride Street, south of the river near Dublin Castle. On Wednesday, too, dispatch carriers were still plying between the various major insurgent posts across the city. Mary McLoughlin was sent to Jacob's with a message for Thomas MacDonagh. On the way back she went round by her house in North King Street where her mother locked her in her bedroom, but she climbed out of the window and made it back to the GPO, only to be sent again to Jacob's on Thursday. This dropping in at home was taken to extremes by Ignatius Callender, who described working as a courier between the Church Street position and the GPO. He went home each night to Sarsfield Quay, where his mother ran a restaurant. ('On the Wednesday morning, having shaved, washed and put on a clean collar, I had breakfast at about 6.15 am in the same room in the Lucan Restaurant as Lieutenant Anderson and an officer of the RDF.') By Thursday, Callendar found it impossible to get back to the GPO but women messengers were still being sent out. Min and Phyllis Ryan spent Wednesday taking messages from the O'Rahilly to the wives of three British officers who were prisoners in the GPO. They had to travel out to the Drumcondra Road. On Wednesday night they managed to make it back to Walter Coles' house, a Sinn Féin meeting point in Mountjoy Square, where they found Mrs Wyse Power. Jennie Wyse Power owned a restaurant in Henry Street (where the Proclamation had been signed), but she had been forced out by the firing. She urged the girls not to go back, but having slept in the back of the house on Wednesday night they snuck back to the GPO in the morning. 'It would be absolutely idiotic not to; if the men were to die, we would too; that is the way we felt.'

Despite the extreme danger on Thursday, with continuous firing from rifles, machine guns and shells, Pearse sent them out again with messages to his mother. Did he really think it was worth risking the lives of these two girls for a family note? This says something about Pearse, no doubt, but also about the kind of hierarchy at work among the Volunteers. It would have been unthinkable for a rank and file Volunteer to have asked for such privileges.

By Wednesday afternoon the O'Connell Street outposts were coming under increasingly violent attack, and they had little enough to answer with. They fortified the tower of the Dublin Bread Company, from where they were sniping at the guns on Trinity College roof, with cases of raisins and currants. Connolly began calling in the outposts south of the GPO. Messages were signalled across O'Connell Street to evacuate Reis's and go to the Hibernian Bank, to evacuate the hospital in Hoyte's and transfer the wounded to the GPO. This occasioned the sight of men racing across the wide street wrapped in mattresses. Down on the quays the outposts at Kelly's and Hopkins were coming under continuous machine-gun fire from the roof of Trinity College: 'We could make little or no reply to this attack, as our garrison possessed only one rifle – the remainder being armed with shot-guns – the only other armament we possessed being bombs.' James Stephens watched the bombardment of Kelly's from the other side of the river:

I counted the report of six different machine guns which played on it. Rifles innumerable and from every sort of place were potting its windows, and at intervals of about half a minute the shells from a heavy gun lobbed in through its windows or thumped mightily against its walls.

For three hours that bombardment continued and the walls stood in a cloud of red dust and smoke. Rifle and machine gun bullets pattered over every inch of it, and, unfailingly the heavy gun pounded its shells through the windows.

But the men from Kelly's were not there. They had crawled through the holes in the walls and joined up with the Metropole. From Hopkins the men made it to the Imperial, aided by a helpful woman in Cathedral Street who directed them through her house and into North Earl Street, where they climbed a ladder into the Imperial buildings.

The insurgents were still planning for a frontal assault on the GPO, and they became convinced that it would be preceded by a gas attack. Cripps was again sent out on Wednesday afternoon for supplies for creating anti-gas solution: 'I was ordered to obtain the necessary chemicals, prepare the solutions and distribute the antidote to the various posts and with instructions on its use. In this I was helped by several volunteers. One pail of solution I brought up to the post where Mick Collins was in charge. Another pail I brought up on the roof.' In the event of an attack the nose and mouth were to be covered with a cloth soaked in the solution. Unfortunately several people thought the pails contained water and drank it. One of these was an outlandish character variously designated as 'The Cuban' (he claimed to have fought in the Mexican war), 'a Spaniard' (he wore a multicoloured woven belt) or 'a Basque', who used the 'vilest language' over the incident. With hindsight it seems unimaginable that the British would have fired gas in the centre of Dublin, but this was rumoured on the government side also. As Mrs Norway related on Friday:

The GPO has such valuable records, etc., and the contents of the safes are so precious, that they will not raze it to the ground if they can help it; but it has so much subterranean space, that would afford cover to thousands of Sinn Féiners, that we hear they are going to fire some 'gas' shells into it and then rush it!

The fear of a gas attack evoked the fighting in Flanders, but it also spoke of the static waiting game they were now in. As an early history of the Rising put it, 'The isolated strategic points which they had seized became so many traps into which they were gradually penned.' In later years this state of siege became part of the story of the GPO as gallant sacrifice. Richard Mulcahy, for example, argued that 'The men that went in had no opportunity of effective and successful soldierly action. They could do nothing but go in and hold their places and stand their ground until the end came. It was the action of a citizen giving away his life in defiance of guns that marks the spirit of Easter Week.'

As the cordon round the GPO tightened, the men prepared to withstand a massed infantry attack with hand grenades and shotguns. Early on Thursday morning Connolly went out to inspect the Metropole outpost, which had now been extended by boring through internal walls as far as Eason's on Middle Abbey Street. Connolly gave instructions to run up a barricade across to the other side of Abbey Street. He was walking about on the pavement when the first shell hit the block. Oscar Traynor recalled:

They were shrapnel shells, and the amazing thing was that instead of bullets coming in it was molten lead, actually molten, which streamed about on the ground when it fell. I was told that the shrapnel was filled with molten wax, the bullets were embedded in wax, and the velocity of the shell through the barrel and through the air caused the mould to melt. As the first of those shells hit the house, the volunteers rushed and told me about them. I rushed up and found an old fellow crawling about on his hands and knees gathering the stuff up as it hardened. I asked him what he was doing and what he intended to do with the stuff. He said "Souvenirs".

Pretty soon the whole block was reduced to ruins by the shelling and nothing remained between the GPO and the guns at Trinity. There was a British machine gun firing up Lower Abbey Street towards Mansfield's, where the men's rifles became so heated they had to use oil from sardine tins to cool them. They were also being fired on from the windows of a building at the junction of D'Olier and Westmoreland Street. 'The stream of bullets from this gun was reducing the wall opposite to a heap of ground up bricks and plaster and filling the room with a choking dust.' Traynor crawled back through the block to the GPO for orders. They were to keep going.

Later that day one of the incendiary shells set fire to the barricade, packed with wooden cases for bicycles, on Lower Abbey Street, opposite the Metropole block. As Traynor remembered:

It was the firing of this barricade that caused the fire which wiped out the east side of O'Connell St. I saw that happen myself. I saw the barricade being hit; I saw the fire consuming it and I saw Keating's going up. Then Hoyt's [sic] caught fire, and when Hoyt's caught fire the whole block up to Earl St. became involved. Hoyt's had a lot of turpentine and other inflammable stuff, and I saw the fire spread from there to Clery's. Clery's and the Imperial Hotel were one and the same building, and this building was ignited by the fire which consumed Hoyt's. Before that happened those of us in the Metropole made tremendous efforts to warn the garrison in the Imperial Hotel of the grave danger which menaced them. If our messages, which were sent by semaphore, were understood they do not appear to have been acted on, as the eventual evacuation of the Imperial Hotel appears to have been a rather hurried one. I had the extraordinary experience of seeing the huge plate-glass windows of Clery's stores run molten into the channel from the terrific heat.

It was now so hot in the GPO that water poured on the defences and barricades turned to steam. Men's hands and faces were scorched red from the heat. The terror now was of being burned alive. About 100 guests in the Gresham had been trapped since Monday. British snipers had commandeered the roof on Tuesday and moved all the guests to the back. Panic grew with the fires: 'All the women were on their knees in the billiard-room saying the Rosary, and the queerest thing of all was to see the English and Scotch ladies, who were Protestants and Presbyterians, down on their knees with the Catholics joining in as far as they knew how.'

It was on Thursday that Leslie Price was sent to the Pro-Cathedral for a priest. She took a circuitous route, up Moore Street and round by the Rotunda, crawling in by the walls as she was 'terrified'. The priest who opened the door to her, Father John Flanagan, was understandably not keen on going back with her to the GPO. He had been anointing the wounded in the streets and in Jervis Street Hospital from Monday to Wednesday, and he had heard confessions in the GPO on Monday. Apart from the danger of the streets, his difficulty was finding a way in to the building. Joseph Cripps had been out again on Thursday morning to get medical supplies when he ran into Father Flanagan, who asked for help getting in:

> I brought him in through the Hall door at the side of Bewleys. The Hall was stacked with foodstuffs, Hams etc. He made quite a fuss about stolen goods. In the P.O. he went around the garrison and visited the wounded. Late in the evening he asked me to get him out. At the time firing was very heavy. We got as far as the floor over McDowell's (Opposite Moore St). Leo Henderson was in charge. An armoured car at the far end of Moore Street was riddling the room with bullets, a large mirror facing the window was shattered to pieces. Slattery at a window was swing [sic] from a sashcord to fire up Moore Street.

Father Flanagan decided to stay (someone helpfully found him a razor and soap the next day). His pockets were full of notes from the rebels to their wives and mothers, and lists of addresses so that he could notify relatives in case they didn't make it, scribbled on the backs of scraps of Post Office paper and envelopes. Some men wrote out their wills for him. One of the London Irish willed his presentation watch to a man in Kentish town, and his presentation cigarette case to a man in Marylebone. On the back of a 'Summary of Lecture on Aiming Instruction' ('Object: To ensure that a man can aim accurately and quickly at an indistinct target, making allowance when necessary for wind or movement') another had written in thick pencil:

£20 to Sister Bee
10 to Sister Maggie
10 to " Mary
5 to ? Hunt
Watch to Brother John
Bicycle to young Tommy Collins
Good Bye
Ed Henry 28-4-16
Will be sent to mother by Fr Flanagan Marlborough
    St.

And up the side of the page, as an afterthought: 'Mother the balance of pay and send £1–10 to Const Moriarty Boyle and J. H. Cos Boyle and ask if I owe him any if so pay Good Bye H xx'.

One letter that Father Flanagan didn't have, because it was taken from a Volunteer in the surrender, was written to 'Dear Mummie' in the Hotel Metropole on Friday:

I'm quite used to being under fire now and have even shaved while big guns were going. I lost my knapsack, but have since got an overcoat and safety razor. Of course there are plenty of blankets and towels and other things here. How is Frank and Tim and everybody else getting on. Tell Rudy Shiels and Lini and the rest I was asking for them. I don't know where Boss Shiels is. I imagine he is at Headquarters, which is of course the G.P.O. over which are flying the Green Flag and the Republican Flag.

According to International Law Ireland is now a Republic, so I expect it won't be long till we get some help from Germany and may be America. I have heard the Irish Brigade from Berlin 3000 strong has landed in the West. We're doing very well here and affairs over the City are satisfactory for us. I suppose you wondered what all the fires were, from the Imperial Hotel to the D.B.C. was on fire, and also was Taafe's [sic] and Lawrence's, I never saw such a sight, I think that James Daly is up at the Four Courts which we hold. I hear Fr. Flanagan is at Headquarters and I am going across to get him to deliver this to you. Fellows are going to Confession to him.

I don't need to as we got absolution on Monday last, in the Fr. Matthew [sic] Park. No casualties at all here, I stop now, I'm going to try and send some money to you, I might be able to get some. I expect it won't be long till you see me again. Pray for me. Best love to all and yourself Mummie. from Charlie.

Both Pearse and Connolly produced bulletins on Friday, aimed at maintaining morale. Pearse praised the gallantry of the men and suggested this was victory in itself: 'If they do not win this fight, they will at least have deserved to win it. But win it they will, although they may win it in death. Already they have won a great thing. They have redeemed Dublin from many shames, and made her name splendid among the names of Cities.' The language of redemption must have seemed necessary in the face of the obvious military failure of the enterprise. The coming rout was to be met bravely, as Pearse announced that the Army of the Republic was 'busy completing arrangements for the final defence of Headquarters, and are determined to hold it while the building lasts'. There was no hope of this message being broadcast beyond the GPO.

Connolly, badly injured in the ankle by a ricochet bullet, had had his leg set by one of the British prisoners, a doctor with the Indian Service who was home on leave. He was now set up on a wheeled couch on the ground floor, as the GPO itself began to catch fire. As Connolly wrote in his final communiqué: 'We are here hemmed in, because the enemy feels that in this building is to be found the heart and inspiration of our great movement.'

The roof of the GPO at the Prince's Street corner was the first to catch light. Men tried to stem the flames with buckets of water, and finally by directing hoses up through the ventilation shafts. By midday the roofers were brought down, along with the men from the upper floors. The prisoners were taken to the basement, ostensibly for their safety, but later they would complain that they were left there for hours like rats in a trap – a situation made worse as grenades and gelignite were also brought to the basement to keep them out of the way of the flames. At this time, too, the majority of the women left – FitzGerald arguing that plates and cutlery were perhaps now unnecessary and the kitchen staff could be reduced to a minimum. Even now the men expected a frontal attack, and much of the morning was spent building an L-shaped barricade, mainly consisting of sacks of coal, across the ground floor of the building.

As evening fell, the fires spread through the building. 'Everyone seems to consider it his duty to give orders at the top of his voice. The noise is terrific. The fire is gaining ground like lightning.' The immediate problem to be faced was what to do with the wounded, most of whom were from the roof. A party including Father Flanagan, the British doctor and most of the remaining women took the wounded to Jervis Street Hospital, by going through the tunnellings and across roofs into the Coliseum. There they found themselves trapped (Father Flanagan tried lowering the safety curtain on the stage to protect the wounded from the fires). The group made a Red Cross flag out of a nurse's apron and a broom handle and broke their way through Prince's Street to Abbey Street, where Father Flanagan and Dr Mahoney went to the British barricade. At Jervis Street the able-bodied men, who had been escorting the wounded, were turned back:

> The enemy then formed up our men and gave orders that I was to take them back – the Comdt. saying that we were going back to where we had come from to be shot or burned out; he gave orders to his sub-ordinates, 'These men who are going out now are not to be fired on until out of sight and out of sight only.'

Some of the men got back to the Coliseum, others to Arnotts, where someone turned the sprinklers on. In Arnotts, a department store, the more canny among them started changing out of their uniforms. ('This explains how Sgt Gleeson of the ICA Red Cross Unit, had on two pairs of pants and no other clothes except a blanket when he was captured by the British.') Several of the Volunteers who had been in outposts in Liffey Street also took the option of lying low, changing out of their Volunteer or ICA uniforms, and mingling with the local residents on Saturday morning.

At seven o'clock in the evening, with the GPO in flames, the bombs were moved again, from the basement to a storeroom off the Prince's Street courtyard. The prisoners were moved from the basement to the rear of the building. At eight o'clock the Volunteers, gathered together on the ground floor, sang 'The Soldier's Song' – something that is made much of in all the rebel accounts. 'Here was an expression of defiance against British power, and of faith that from the ashes of the doomed GPO would rise the independent Ireland for which they had fought.'

The final evacuation of the GPO took place in stages. There were three main parties. Soon after 8 pm about thirty or forty men formed up in two lines and attempted to charge down Moore Street, under the command of the O'Rahilly. The British were firing from a barricade at the end of Moore Street and many were wounded or killed, including the O'Rahilly. Others crouched in doorways or in houses. A party of men hid in Williams' factory in Sampson's Lane and another got into a house in Moore Street.

At 8.30 the prisoners – about fifteen of them – were given the choice of running for it from the Henry Street entrance, or staying. Afterwards the rebels would be accused of sending men running to their deaths, as the British were firing from barricades on Henry Street and Moore Street.

Ten minutes later the main evacuation began. The aim was to try to break through to the north of the city. 'Pearse stood at the exit sword in hand. Every so often he dropped the sword as the signal for two more men to leave and make the short dash across Henry Street. We all got over safely into Moore Lane.' This – James Ryan's description – was hardly an accurate reflection of the panic and danger. Men dashed as well as they could across to Henry Place, crouching in doorways and trapped in courtyards. Connolly was carried on a makeshift stretcher. Sean McLaughlin recalled:

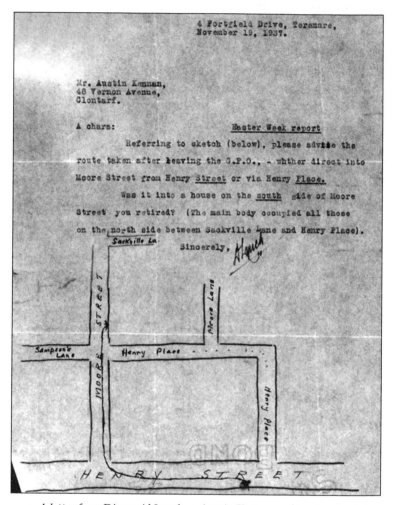

4 Fortfield Drive, Terenure,
November 19, 1937.

Mr. Austin Kennan,
46 Vernon Avenue,
Clontarf.

A chara: Easter Week report

          Referring to sketch (below), please advise the
route taken after leaving the G.P.O., - whther direct into
Moore Street from Henry Street or via Henry Place.

          Was it into a house on the south side of Moore
Street you retired? (The main body occupied all those
on the north side between Sackville Lane and Henry Place).

Sincerely,

9. *A letter from Diarmuid Lynch to Austin Kennan, asking him to plot
the route taken by the O'Rahilly's men in their charge from the building.
Kennan's drawing shows the men running down Moore Street, and therefore
directly towards a British barricade, rather than through Henry Place, which
was the route taken by the men in the final evacuation.*

We were opposite Moore Lane when there was a terrific blaze of fire from the far end and we realised that the British were in possession of the barricades. I turned back towards the Post Office and saw the whole garrison coming towards me at a run. There was terrible confusion – almost panic. No one seemed to have any idea what to do. Somebody shouted that we were being fired on from the roof of a mineral water factory. I detailed a number of men to break the door down. Another party entered from the opposite door and they opened fire on each other – one man was killed and several wounded. I was incensed with rage calling 'Have you gone mad – what the hell is wrong!' and I drove them towards the wall threatening them.

Eventually the men broke into a shop at the corner of Moore Street and Henry Place and from there they started tunnelling, yet again, through the houses towards Parnell Street. Parties of men crawled through the walls, dragging Connolly with them. 'We took him through holes linking the houses towards the GHQ in the middle of the street. Some of the holes were on the ground floor, some on the first floor, and the stairways were narrow. All in all Connolly had a gruelling time and was in great pain.' At midday on Saturday the leaders, ensconced in a house in Moore Street and increasingly disturbed by the civilian deaths around them, took the decision to surrender.

For the insurgents it was nearly over. It took some time to contact all of the rebel positions across the city, and even then solitary gunmen continued sniping for several days on the rooftops in areas south of the river. Some of the insurgents managed to escape, but for the majority the near future was to be spent in English prisons and internment camps. For the leaders there was no future at all; fifteen of the leaders were executed by firing squad between the third and the twelfth of May.

On Thursday, 27 April in London, General Sir John Maxwell was appointed Commander-in-Chief of the British troops in Ireland, and he became the main force behind the British government's response to the Rising. Arriving in Dublin on Friday 28th, he had full authority to restore order, suppress the Rising and punish the insurgents, assuming the role of military governor under martial law. Maxwell was determined to counter what he regarded as the weakness of the civil administration, under Chief Secretary Birrell, which he felt had been responsible for encouraging sedition and lawlessness. By 30 April, two days after his arrival, around 1,000 people had been arrested and nearly half that number were on their way to detention centres in England. The next weeks would see more than 3,000 people rounded up, 183 courts martial and 90 death sentences. As many historians have argued, within a few weeks the political landscape in Ireland was completely transformed in response to the perceived brutality of Maxwell's crackdown. On the Sunday after Easter week, however, as the rebels were still being rounded up, the residents of Dublin seem to have greeted the end of the Rising philosophically. 'Needless to say,' explained Thomas King Moylan, 'there is a great relief at the quick ending of the rising, and at the same time a feel [sic] as if the holidays are over.'

Two responses recurred in observers' accounts and diaries of the end of the week, both of them bound up with the war on the Western Front. The first focused on how the slaughter on the Continent had affected ordinary people's ability to respond to the deaths around them. People were shocked to find themselves laughing in the midst of the violence, or worrying about the milk supply. James Stephens described the feeling as the loss of the 'morbidity' of death. The fear of death, he argued, had subsided because of the European war. Among other things, Stephens hazarded that this meant there would be nothing to stop further armed protests. Thomas King Moylan argued that the war had 'inured ordinary people to violence'. Mrs Hamilton Norway (whose eldest son had been killed in France only months before) was surprised at the total absence of thankfulness for escape. 'Life as it has been lived for the last two years in the midst of death seems to have blunted one's desire for it, and completely changed one's feelings about the Hereafter.'

It has become common to set Pearse's invocations of blood sacrifice, now so alien to us, in the context of the patriotic rhetoric of the European war. But a year before the Rising, in one of his most sombre essays, Freud had provided a different slant. The pervasiveness of death in the war had dislocated the 'civilized' attitude to death – that it was an unfortunate accident, best not mentioned in polite company. Europeans were being forced to view dying as primeval man had regarded it, as an ever-present part of life. But this attitude, Freud thought, had an almost schizophrenic flip side: 'Life has, indeed, become interesting again; it has recovered its full content.' The very ordinariness of death encouraged the urge towards the heroic transcendence of life. What these observers noticed about the disturbing new ordinariness of death is likely to have also been true of the participants in the Rising. The Volunteers' willingness to die for their ideals may have had as much to do with the inevitability and closeness of death during the war as with heroic patriotism. As

Min Ryan had put it, 'if the men were to die, we would too; that is the way we felt.'

The other response among eyewitnesses was an even more direct comparison with the Continent. It is hard to find any single account of the Rising that does not set Dublin beside Ypres and Louvain – whether to prove the brutality of the government forces, to bring home the horror of what the city had been through, or to suggest the chance for a miniature experience of the Western Front. Mrs Hamilton Norway wrote to her relatives: 'If you look at pictures of Ypres or Louvain after the bombardment it will give you some idea of the scene ... If at all possible you ought to come over for Whitsuntide. You will see such a sight as you will never see in your life unless you go to Belgium.' The scenes of destruction were a kind of physical manifestation of the rebels' hopeless stand against the Empire, and may offer a further clue to the currency of the idea of being wiped out. Ypres, after all, was known to the British as 'Wipers', as in the A to Z of the Rising quickly doing the rounds of the Dublin streets:

Y for New Ypres, which stands on the Liffey,
By British Huns shelled to the ground in a jiffy.

3

RECONSTRUCTION

*'One man can free a people as one man redeemed the world.
I will take no pike. I will go into battle with bare hands. I
will stand up before the Gall as Christ hung naked before
men on a tree.'*

Patrick Pearse, *The Singer*

*'Looking at it from the inside (I was in the G.P.O.) it had the
air of a Greek tragedy about it.'*

Michael Collins

In a West London music hall, on the evening that the first
news of the rebellion was published in London, the audience
were treated to a rousing feel-good finale: an emotional rendition of the popular song 'When British Eyes Are Smiling'.
As one member of the audience explained, 'The news had
just come through, popular indignation against Ireland ran
high, and no one knew how much of the truth had got into
the papers. There was a widespread belief that Ireland was
full of Germans who, after massacring all the English soldiers in Dublin and the rest of Ireland, would proceed to
swoop on London.' Against this volatile background the
singer decided that the programme's closing number, with
its syrupy chorus, 'When Irish hearts are happy/All the

world seems bright and gay', would be asking too much of his audience.

Precisely because English stereotypes of the Irish were so suffused with sentimentalism – allowing the strains of 'It's a Long Way to Tipperary' to send so many off to the Front – they could tip easily into the caricature of the two-faced and aggressive ingrate. The immediate response to news of the Rising in Britain was that it was treacherous and low-down of the Irish, but no more than was to be expected. While some reporters emphasised the tiny rebel numbers in comparison to the vast majority of 'loyal' citizens of Empire, and argued that the rank and file had been the 'dupes' of a uniquely corrupting leadership, for the most part the conservative press revelled in the evidence of treachery supplied by the Rising, castigated Birrell, Chief Secretary for Ireland, for his weakness in allowing Irish disloyalty to prosper and praised the severity of General Maxwell's response. Within a couple of weeks of the Rising, Maxwell had extended martial law, overseen the executions of the leaders and supervised the round-up and deportation of thousands of 'Sinn Féiners', many of whom had had nothing to do with the Rising, or, like Eoin MacNeill, had even opposed it.

But there were other, less obvious effects on public opinion in Britain. For a start the reports, photographs and newsreels showing the devastation in Dublin brought the average Englishman and -woman face to face with the events. For a week or two, Ireland was as actual as Belgium, indeed more so. It was not until later that summer that the first full-length documentary film of the war, *The Battle of the Somme*, was shown in cinemas in England, giving rise to impassioned debate on the morality of showing the dead and disaster to the public, as well as feeding fascination with the war itself. But in April 1916 short films and newsreels from the Front were still highly censored. The newsreels from Ireland in the immediate aftermath of the Rising, while they did not show any dead, lingered over dramatic pictures of the ruins, and queues of women and children without food, a familiar landscape made strange by war. In newspapers, too, the suddenness and speed of the events in Dublin, dramatically recounted by civilian eyewitnesses, contrasted sharply with official, censored and euphemistic accounts of hard-to-imagine battles such as Loos, Gallipoli and Verdun. *The Times* published sketchy reports on Dublin on Thursday 27 and Friday 28 April. From the 29th, however, the pages were crammed with eyewitness reports (often three or four at a time) and articles on different aspects of the situation. There were maps of Dublin city centre, copies of the Proclamation and various bulletins, photos of O'Connell Street before and after the shelling, and diagrams of expanding bullets. The editorial on the 29th was fairly dispassionate, even commending the organisation and planning of the Rising and particularly the fact that the rebels had paid for provisions taken from the hotels to the GPO. A week later, reports (several of which were written by the editor of the *Irish Times*) tended to be headlined 'The Butchery of Civilians' and 'Callous Rebels'; the stories were of shooting people in the back, looting, treason:

> An Austrian officer wearing the uniform of his country surrendered at the Post Office when it was set on fire, and is now a prisoner in Dublin Castle. Two Austrians were arrested in a house in the Balls-bridge area; they had been engaged in making bombs.

But beyond the propaganda value of the Rising, it was the ease of access to information and to photographic images that made the difference in reporting events in Dublin. There was just so much of it: reports, tales of lucky escapes, photographs. The *Illustrated London News* was owned by Clement Shorter, whose wife Dora Sigerson was an Irishwoman and a nationalist. Shorter's business head meant he kept any overt rebel-friendly opinions out of the paper. Yet the double-page spreads of the devastation in Dublin, and portraits of key personalities, contrasted sharply with the usual indistinct and puzzling photographs of blasted landscapes in France. As one commentator wrote, 'in retrospect the Dublin revolt appeared already as easily the most dramatic episode in a war which in some respects has been one of the dullest in history.'

Ireland's moment in the spotlight wasn't to last. The Rising was soon relegated to a minor interlude, as unsmiling British eyes turned quickly to the surrender at Kut in Mesopotamia, the reversal at Verdun and later the overwhelming casualty lists and grinding hopelessness of the Somme. Gaining the attention of the British public had never meant gaining their sympathy. Nonetheless, according to some accounts, in the weeks that followed the executions the British public's faith in the conduct of the war was shaken. The pacifist and socialist English writer Douglas Goldring argued in 1917 that the contrast between the courageous behaviour of the rebels and the brutality of the army (particularly the killing of Sheehy Skeffington and two other civilians in Portobello Barracks) caused revulsion:

There was something bungling and ignoble in the whole proceeding … What a contrast to all this seemed the behaviour of the rebel leaders! They were foolish, insane as it appears to us, but insanely honest and sincere. Nothing ignoble or mean or (according to their lights) ungenerous, has ever been proved against them. The inevitable reaction in England in their favour when the truth gradually emerged was very strong, and its influence is still felt ... The necessity to win through to an honourable peace has not been weakened by it; but the old confidence that we were the champions of small nations, that ours was a 'Holy War', that we could never succumb to 'militarism' has received a shock.

Debate over the Rising in both Britain and Ireland was later to focus almost exclusively on its political logic: the question of whether it was better to have taken an insurrectionary or constitutional route to political change in Ireland, whether it should be understood as social revolution, putsch or the kickstart for democracy in Ireland. Initial responses to the Rising were much more varied, however. The conduct of the war, debates about patriotism, the impact of socialist and left internationalist ideas: all played a part in how the Rising was interpreted in those first months. One issue which the Rising seemed to illuminate was the debate about British militarism. And the idea that the rebels had fought a 'clean' and honourable fight against increasingly militarist imperial forces was later able to feed quite naturally into the story of willing sacrifice for the nation.

Along with others wishing to make political capital out of any protest against the war, Goldring certainly overstated the amount of British sympathy with the rebels. But he didn't entirely make it up. Where there was shocked reaction against the behaviour of the British troops – of the kind so often replicated in reports of brutality in more recent wars – it was in part a consequence of the increasing gap between the rhetoric of honour and bravery and the realities of modern warfare. At this point in the war, reports from the Front still clung to an earlier rhetoric of individual action and power, of heroism, even as the casualty lists grew. It wasn't simply the techniques of the war that had been brought home to Dublin – the use of artillery rather than cavalry, the shoulder-to-shoulder advances which prefigured the Somme – but the dehumanising effects of mechanised violence.

By the standards of 1916, Dublin got off lightly in terms of physical damage and casualties. This was much more a colonial-style repression than a Western Front-style bombardment, though arguably it was so only because the rebels surrendered. Yet within weeks the main story for the British anti-war lobby was of the disproportionate use of force by their own side. One story of dishonourable British conduct that was recounted in Ireland, and published in the tiny anti-war press in Britain, was of how the rebels fleeing from the burning GPO had been tricked into running down Henry Place, and then machine-gunned after they had passed the bend in the road.

While for mainstream British public opinion Irish treachery and German atrocity were pretty much synonymous in the aftermath of the Rising, small groups of socialists and pacifists in Britain made what propaganda they could out of the events. As early as 6 May (before the executions were over) the feminist and pacifist Sylvia Pankhurst decried the unequal force used against the rebels, arguing that the poor conditions in Dublin and the rest of country accounted for the revolt: 'The rebels – judge them who can find heart to do so – well knew by their reckless bravery that they would be

defeated, that their rebellion was but a stage in the long struggle for Irish independence.' Pankhurst had broken with her
mother and sister, Emmeline and Christabel Pankurst, over
their support for the war, and launched her own breakaway
suffragette organisation, the Workers Socialist Federation.
Her journal the *Woman's Dreadnought* published a series of
articles attacking British militarism in Ireland. The aim was
to downplay the aspects of the Rising that smacked of the
militarist coup, and to reveal the hollowness of the wartime
rhetoric of British honour pitted against German brutality:

> ... all the harm this handful of patriots could do would
> be as nothing when compared with the dastardly deed of
> the English Government, which had Dublin shelled by
> machine guns, and was only held back from razing it to
> the ground – as the Germans did the Belgian towns – by
> the surrender of the patriots.

The trick of representing the rebels as peaceful patriots
was undoubtedly helped by the murder of the crusadingly
pacifist Sheehy Skeffington. One article on the 'brave rebel
boys' in the *Woman's Dreadnought* was by Sir Francis Fletcher
Vane, the major who was sacked after blowing the whistle
on Captain Bowen-Colthurst, the deranged officer responsible for the Portobello Barracks killings. As the suffragist
and trade unionist Louie Bennett argued, 'his story ringing
through the length and breadth of Ireland, and much further
afield, was doing more to weaken the prestige of the militarist system than years of propaganda could do'. The murders
were taken up in English radical journals such as the Christian pacifist periodical *Truth*, where they were used to prove
the innate barbarism of war:

Possibly everybody had more or less lost their heads: but they must have been nearly as mad as the captain if they did not see that he was bent on cold-blooded murder, and that their duty was to stop him, even at some risk to themselves. If he had ordered the firing party to shoot one another, or to shoot him, would they have done it? It almost looks like it. And we have so many novices in the Army it might be as well if some general instructions were issued to troops, explaining that military discipline does not require them to commit crimes at the word of command. Otherwise a general may go off his head and order his troops to attack and destroy the nearest town, and the thing will be done.

On the face of it there was little in common between the armed Volunteers and the anti-war movement in Britain, where pacifism was largely religious in orientation. Desmond Ryan (who was in the GPO) recalled that when his party of prisoners turned up at Wakefield prison they were jeered at by a group of conscientious objectors. The warder yelled back at the COs that at least the volunteers had had the courage to fight for their country.

But despite the ideological clash between militarism and pacifism there is some evidence of mutual support between the groups. In fact one of the oddest consequences of the rebels' military action was that within a few months of the Rising Sinn Féin was able to represent itself as the party of peace, attracting war-weary voters. The insurgents, after all, had risen in protest against Irish involvement in the war. Left-wing intellectuals in Britain, such as those associated with *The Nation* and the *New Statesman* and with the Union of Democratic Control, were ready to make what they could of it.

Support for the Rising in Britain reached its height in the wake of the February revolution in Russia. This galvanised members of the Union of Democratic Control into thinking the time might be right for a mass movement against the war. In April 1917 Bertrand Russell wrote to Ottoline Morrell after a mass meeting of anti-war groups at the Albert Hall: 'There was a lot said about Ireland – the Sinn Fein martyrs were enthusiastically cheered – the Russians have really put a new spirit into the world, and it is going to be worth while to be alive.' The argument was not so much that Ireland had moved too early, as Lenin suggested, but that it was the natural vanguard for the coming revolution. Drawing up a template for a 'British Charter of Freedom' (modelled on the Russian example), Russell listed their demands in the following order:

1 Release of Irish prisoners, and of conscientious objectors.
2 Cessation of prosecutions under the Defence of the Realm Act (DORA).
3 Home Rule; also the right of asylum.
4 Adult Suffrage.

His companion list of those who could be counted on to support the campaign began with 'The Irish'.

It wouldn't do to overstate the degree of this support. In the main, British left and liberal responses to the Rising were uncertain, or downright hostile. Connolly's nationalist zeal made him a decidedly flawed hero for international social- ists, and the numerous British and Scottish socialist parties tended to come out against him. The Independent Labour Party, the British Socialist Party, the Socialist Labour Party

of Britain: all lamented Connolly's seemingly inexplicable
decision to throw in his lot with a bunch of bourgeois nationalists, even while they blamed the government's refusal to
face down Carson and the Ulster Volunteer Force for creating the situation. Elements within the Labour Party and
the British Trades Union Congress openly condemned the
Rising. Things were awkward for the Labour Party, since the
British wartime coalition included several Labour MPs in
government. Even if they had wished to speak out in favour
of the labour aspect of the Rising they could not have done
so. Yet criticisms of British militarism did surface in socialist and pacifist journals. Arguably they were to have their
greatest impact a few years later during the Irish War of
Independence, when the British government was to lose the
propaganda battle for the role of defender of small nations,
in part because of the ruthless behaviour of the Black and
Tans and the Auxiliary occupying forces in Ireland.

🁣

There was a large amount of wishful thinking in the claim
that the Rising dented Britain's faith in its military mien, but
in Ireland the nobility of the rebels' action quickly became
the acceptable mode for talking about the Rising. Here again
the initial emphasis was on the clash between mechanised
militarism and the honour and bravery shown by the rebel
soldiers. Commentators continually stressed their bravery
against overwhelming odds. As one correspondent to a provincial newspaper put it: 'There were no stags or skulkers
amongst them. They stood by each other to the last. Hence a
great wave of sympathy has gone out to their memory from
every true Irish heart ... They loved their country not at all

wisely, but too well.' The rebels might have been crazed Othellos, destroying the thing they loved, but at least they weren't cowards.

The shadow of Victorian heroic rhetoric falls across accounts of the rebels as of their counterparts in the British army. On 11 May, John Dillon, of the Irish Parliamentary Party, made the comparison explicit in an impassioned speech to the House of Commons condemning the executions:

> It is not murderers who are being executed; it is insurgents who have fought a clean fight, a brave fight, however misguided, and it would be a damned good thing for you if your soldiers were able to put up as good a fight as did those men in Dublin – three thousand men against twenty thousand with machine guns and artillery.

This speech, which shocked the House, has often been quoted as proof that even those most hurt by the Rising were able to praise the courage of the rebels, though they deplored their actions. A parliamentary colleague who met Dillon around this time described him as 'black with suppressed passion'. He was deeply frustrated with the government, and in particular with Maxwell, as he believed that martial law, the executions and imprisonments, were driving moderate Irishmen away from their trust in the constitutional party.

But Dillon's House of Commons speech was equally remarkable for the insights it gave into his view of the war with Germany. He spluttered over 'your soldiers', but 'your soldiers' already included many Irishmen, who had joined up because of assurances by Dillon and his leader Redmond that this was the surest way to secure Home Rule. Thousands had seen devastating combat at Suvla Bay in Gallipoli and on the Western Front. During the week of the Rising, 570 men of the 16th (Irish) Division were killed at Hulloch in Belgium, and 1,400 were gassed and wounded. It was not that Dillon was doubting the courage of the men at the Front. Rather he was trying to get across to the House how many more might have joined them if Britain's Irish policy had been wiser, and if Home Rule had already been introduced. But what is most striking is that the language of the clean and brave fight (rather than the hopeless endurance of the horror of the trenches) was still available to him.

Dillon's fears that the moderate nationalism of the Irish Parliamentary Party was losing ground in the wake of the executions were correct. The swift changes of public opinion charted in James Stephens' diary of events reveal the volatility of the situation. A day or two after the end of the Rising, Stephens could write to his British readers that 'There is no bitterness in Ireland against you on account of this war, and the lack of ill-feeling amongst us is entirely due to the more than admirable behaviour of the soldiers whom you sent over here.' Arguing that there was a real possibility for peace, he blamed Redmond and the Irish Parliamentary Party for misrepresenting the Irish people in pledging their support for the war. It was this kind of sentiment that spooked moderate nationalists.

And ill-feeling against the British was growing fast under martial law. For nine days during the secret trials the public heard of executions without any account of the proceedings or the evidence that had been presented. There were no defence lawyers; political status was refused to the prisoners; curfew was enforced; there were regular house searches and arrests. Dillon had spent two weeks assessing the damage. He found Dublin seething with rumours about secret executions and what was going on inside the military barracks. The force of the Sheehy Skeffington incident lay not only in the shock that it had happened, but in the fear that it may happen again, or had already happened. Many people were convinced it was merely the tip of an iceberg. There were rumours that a huge pit had been dug at Arbour Hill to take hundreds of bodies. On 7 May Dillon had written to Redmond urging him once more to lobby the Prime Minister to put a stop to the executions: 'Rumours are circulating and are widely believed that a large number have been shot without trial.'

As the weeks passed the stories of bravery became paramount, the fearless men though few. There were no skulkers among the rebels, no cowards, no one who changed their mind. It was as though the analogy between the Irish and the Greeks, laid out in Thomas Davis's immensely popular nineteenth-century song 'A Nation Once Again', had suddenly borne fruit.

> When boyhood's fire was in my blood,
> I read of ancient freemen,
> For Greece and Rome who bravely stood,
> Three hundred men and three men.

Or, as Dillon put it, three thousand.

Admittedly the idea of the GPO as an Irish Thermopylae was a stretch. Yet the fact that the Rising ended in a last stand in the Post Office meant that it could be read as a defensive battle against a far more powerful enemy. The hopelessness of the rebels' stand was later used, ad nauseam, to argue that the Rising was all along intended as a blood sacrifice designed to rejuvenate a moribund national consciousness. Yet it arose initially from the real and sudden clash between the might and methods of modern warfare, and the rhetoric of nobility and idealism in which soldiering was still couched. This had been a shock for Pearse, Connolly and many of the rebels themselves, and as the secret courts martial and executions continued – like watching a stream of blood coming from beneath a closed door, said one observer – it was a shock for the Irish in general. Those who stressed the courage of the rebels were not simply sentimentalists who were blind to the horrific disproportion between the carnage on the Western Front and the events in Dublin. The emphasis on courage and bravery was an echo of the wartime rhetoric of honour – the most obvious language available in which to express sympathy. Writing in the London *Daily News* on 10 May, even Bernard Shaw employed the language of fair play:

> My own view is that the men who were shot in cold blood, after their capture or surrender, were prisoners of war, and that it was, therefore, entirely incorrect to slaughter them ... I remain an Irishman and am bound to contradict any implication that I can regard as a traitor any Irishman taken in a fight for Irish independence against the British government, which was a fair fight in everything except the enormous odds my countrymen had to face.

It is a commonplace that while the Rising itself garnered little support among the Irish in general, the executions and wholesale round-up and imprisonment of suspects turned the tide of sympathy in favour of the rebels. Not surprisingly, many of the rebels themselves rejected this line, arguing instead that the insurrection itself, rather than the executions, acted as a catalyst for the growing support for Sinn Féin. This was, in effect, a version of the 'heroic gesture' which both Pearse and Connolly had fallen back on in the last days and hours in the Post Office. In the months before the Rising the leaders may have anticipated a nationwide revolt, with the aid of German arms, but by the end of Easter week the justification for the Rising had contracted to the effect that by taking up arms the rebels had saved Ireland's honour. What is remarkable is that within a few weeks this view had gained common currency. By 8 May, James Stephens, who could by no means have been described as a radical republican, was expressing almost identical sentiments: 'The blood of brave men had to sanctify such a consummation if the national imagination was to be stirred to the dreadful business which is the organising of freedom, and both imagination and brains have been stagnant in Ireland this many a year.'

This shift in perspective was everywhere apparent. Initial responses to the Rising published in both national and provincial Irish newspapers on Saturday, 29 April were informed in almost equal parts by rumour and prejudice. For the most part the Rising was condemned as a German plot, with the fear of German invasion uppermost (helmets appearing over the hedges). This clearly followed Redmond's line that the rebellion sprang not from Irish roots but was planned and instigated by Germany. It was condemned as 'insane and criminal' by the conservative press. It had been masterminded in Dublin by socialists influenced by the trades unionists James Larkin and James Connolly; it was a stab in the back for Home Rule.

Yet little more than a week later (following the first of the executions) readers were being encouraged to view the rebels as foolish but courageous; 'brave if misguided men', according to the *Kilkenny People*. The *Westmeath Independent* drew the comparison with the courage shown on the Western Front: 'These young men are Irishmen. They are the class from whom has been drawn the Irish soldier, who has made the world ring with his valour.'

It was at this point that more detailed news coverage began to get through to areas outside Dublin, including news of the Portobello Barracks murders, and accusations that British soldiers had shot innocent civilians in North King Street. The charge against the British for their brutality focused not on the executions but on the suppression of the rebellion itself. The young socialist, and future children's novelist, Patricia Lynch arrived in Dublin three days after the end of the rebellion when, despite the rain, the ruins of the GPO still smouldered. The accusation of unfairness was already strong, as the German analogy quickly shifted from the rebels (treacherously in league with Germany) to the British (twinned with the Germans in their brutality). The link would later be fixed as 'Britannia's Huns with their long range guns'. Lynch found complaints of the amount of ammunition used – as much 'for one sniper as would wipe out a German regiment' – and claims that as far as wholesale destruction went, 'The Germans could not do worse!'

'They tell us to pity the Belgians; it's ourselves need pity, I'm thinking.' The affair at the Post Office aroused great horror: 'To turn machine guns on them and they running away!' 'The English papers talk of Louvain; what'll they say of Dublin?'

Although there were still those who condemned the revolution because of the inconveniences it had caused, Lynch found people everywhere drawing the contrast between the purity and romanticism of the rebels (displayed in technicolour by Grace Gifford's marriage to Plunkett the night before his execution) and the unfair arrests and imprisonment. The focus was on the insurgents' clean and brave fight, their impeccable behaviour (no drinking, for example) and the tragic dignity of the leaders facing death. 'I saw that in Ireland the attitude towards the rebels taken by many, even of those who condemn the rising, is one of esteem, admiration and love.'

Irish public opinion was not so much reversed as crystallised by the combination of the executions and better information about the events in Dublin. People out on the streets during the rebellion itself had been struck by the general reticence: opinion on the rights and wrongs of the Rising was volatile, and many people preferred to wait and see before they came out strongly either way. By the end of May, opinion had settled on the rebels' bravery. As one British commentator put it: 'The sympathies of the ordinary Irish are with Sinn Fein. They want independence and their only criticism of the rebellion is that it was foolish (not criminal or otherwise wrong), but just foolish because it had no chance of success.'

⧗

The finest part of our city has been blown to smithereens, and burned into ashes. Soldiers amongst us who have served abroad say that the ruin of this quarter is more complete than anything they have seen at Ypres, than anything they have seen anywhere in France or Flanders.

10. A postcard of the ruined GPO, showing people sifting through the rubble of the public office. The shape of the arched glass roof is still visible above the pillars, but the Telephone Silence Cabinet has gone.

It is true that not everyone lamented the destruction of the city. Bernard Shaw wrote to the *New Statesman* on 6 May arguing that 'It is greatly to be regretted that so very little of Dublin has been demolished. The General Post Office was a monument, fortunately not imperishable, of how extremely dull eighteenth-century pseudo-classic architecture can be. Its demolition does not matter. What does matter is that all the Liffey slums have not been abolished.' We could read this as an ironic statement of support for Connolly's class warfare. Shaw was exposing the fetish of property that lay at the heart of the British establishment. It is fair to say that most people did not see it that way.

Nonetheless, in assessing the change of attitude towards

the rebels we should not underestimate the effect of the ruins. Comparisons with Ypres and Louvain came from both sides, to prove either the criminality of the British, using heavy guns in the centre of the city, or the criminality of the rebels for starting the thing. O'Connell Street very quickly became a tourist site – the postcards showed not only ruins but tourists inspecting them, searching for souvenirs. Mrs Hamilton Norway had urged her relatives to cross to Dublin as soon as they could. In relative safety they could get a feel for the destruction on the Continent. Katherine Tynan travelled up from Mayo at the first opportunity: 'In the days that followed we went over all the ground of the Rebellion.' They were motivated by curiosity. But for many Dubliners the ruins were swiftly transformed into a site of pilgrimage. They were looking not for souvenirs but for relics.

In the weeks following the executions, Dublin streets became a theatre for showing sympathy and support for the rebels. Songs and badges were an antidote to the repressions of martial law, and were very hard to police. The shops were full of Rising memorabilia: postcards, Mass cards, song sheets, pamphlets, flags, badges, pictures, photograph albums, calendars. Many of these items were mass-produced by Sinn Féin, making the most of the opportunities for propaganda. But for the people who bought them more was at stake than political posturing – they were invested with an emotional charge. Douglas Goldring arrived in Dublin at the end of May:

> Picture postcards of the executed rebels were displayed in almost every shop window, and their faces were gazed upon with silent veneration by the passers-by ... Up and down Sackville Street urchins ran selling broad sheets

11 This example of Rising memorabilia, by Francis Rigney, brings together photographs of the leaders; the major sites of the rebellion, including the GPO; a copy of the Proclamation and the music and words of the 1798 rebel song, rewritten for the Rising. The figure on the left is a 1798 rebel and on the right is a 1916 Volunteer.

purporting to contain 'The last and inspiring speech of Thomas MacDonagh' ... So far as one could tell, except among the shopkeepers who had not received compensation for their losses and among the upper classes, all resentment against the Sinn Feiners had died away.

At a festival of Irish music in the Father Mathew Hall, Tynan watched the child competitors 'wearing the yellow, white, and green, oddly, in many cases, side by side with the regimental button of a soldier father.' Children played 'the rebels' camp' among the ruins, and sang the new version of the 1798 ballad 'Who Fears to Speak of Easter Week'. The man cleaning Tynan's windows at the Shelbourne Hotel whistled the tune, managing to evade censure while displaying his political opinions at the same time. Churches were full to bursting at the Month's Minds for the dead leaders, one of the first opportunities for sympathisers to come out into the open in some force.

By June, Maxwell was reporting the change of sympathy in Ireland and noting the large numbers of people wearing the Sinn Féin mourning badge: 'They now think that Sinn Feinism and Irish patriotism are synonymous terms.' What Maxwell was witnessing was the effects of the mass arrests, which impinged on many more people than the round-up of the rebels who had actually fought. In wearing badges and carrying flags they were showing their solidarity with those who had been imprisoned. This in itself was a remarkable shift. When the tricolour had been run up on the roof of the GPO on Easter Monday most people had never seen it before, and wondered what it signified. The last Sunday in June was designated Irish flag day, as Goldring explained, 'when collections were being made for the dependants of the rebels and the deportees. Quite fifty per cent of the people one met in the streets on this day were wearing the Republican colours, and the sums collected in the little cardboard boxes must have been considerable. I never saw anyone refuse to give.' As Madge Callanan wrote to James Ryan, then a prisoner in England, 'You have all become great heroes now … You never saw such wholesale conversion.'

Conversion was apposite – the rebels were being recast as

saints. The flag day collections were taken after the Requiem Masses for the Rising dead. If anyone had doubted Pearse's equation of patriotism with holiness the Requiem Masses set them right, with a heady mixture of Christian, nationalist and anti-British rhetoric:

> As the blood of martyrs is the seed of Christians, the blood of patriots is the seed of freedom. It was shed not without hope and it left hope behind, the hope that from it will spring the resurrection of the Spiritual and National Ideals that St Patrick had fused into one; the hope that some day, not far distant, the Churches of St. Patrick will sing a Mass, not of Requiem, but of Thanksgiving, for the establishment of Peace and Freedom in the land to which he brought the liberty of Christ.
>
> Not yet can we get the true perspective, but all signs foreshadow, that in the blood of these men will be written the Epitaph of Robert Emmet.
>
> Whether rash or wise, whether of the weak and foolish that confound the strong, they were of a class and character worthy to break the bonds of a spiritual nation.

The nobility of the leaders was contrasted with the ruthless repression of a system 'that had hanged, burned and shot countless Catholics of England and Ireland'. The rebels by contrast 'hated no-one but loved their land and their people'. They worked for 'the triumph of the spiritual ideal over the unrighteous materialistic system that was strangling it, and [they] bravely died that their nation might live. It will live. The blood of such men is not wasted.' Within a few weeks of the Rising the idea of blood sacrifice was being propounded from altars across the country,

12. *In this popular print,* His Easter Offering, *the rebels' sacrifice for the motherland is cast in the style of a religious pietá. The angel blesses the dying rebel who is supported by the praying figure of Ireland, draped in the tricolour.*

as the Catholic Church responded swiftly to the popular mood and in effect co-opted the rebels' secular martyrdom for itself. The socialist and republican aspects of the Rising were downplayed; the rebels had died for a Catholic nation. Homilies brought together Pearse's own rhetoric of sacrifice with the events as they had unfolded in Easter week, so that the brave but hopeless stand in the GPO became part of the rebels' plan. Pearse had foreseen it all, and he had already made explicit the analogy between the sacrifice of the rebels for the nation and that of Christ for all humanity: 'One man can free a people as one man redeemed the world. I will take no pike. I will go into battle with bare hands. I will stand up before the Gall as Christ hung naked before men on a tree.'

Christian imagery of sacrifice, redemption and resurrection was widespread throughout European public discourse about the fallen of the Great War, offering hope that death could be transcended, and perhaps helping to overcome the fear of death and dying. The cult of the fallen soldier emphasised the spirit of sacrifice in the trenches. English war cemeteries favoured the Cross of Sacrifice as a symbol for their national dead; war memorials in Catholic churches throughout Europe often took the form of a *pietà*, a young soldier in the arms of Christ or Mary. The beatification of the battlefield dead was not a specifically Irish phenomenon, though it took a remarkably strong hold in Ireland. Pearse's fusion of religious and patriotic rhetoric was quickly recast in a specifically Catholic mould. He had been fascinated by the early Irish hero Cuchulainn – an Irish version of the hero willing to sacrifice himself in a battle against overwhelming odds. But it took some time for Cuchulainn to take centre stage in GPO symbolism. For the time being, Christ was far more important. In July 1916 the *Catholic Bulletin* acknowledged the importance of the Requiem Masses in drawing the public together:

> Easter week and its sequel occupy the minds of us all. Elsewhere the story is told in part. The time has not yet come to write it in full. This, however, can be said from independent testimony that history does not record a cleaner fight than that fought by the Volunteers. Another landmark has been fixed in the course of our history. Another epoch has opened. Whatever the future has in store, no-one who knows anything of the country can fail to see that the founts of our nationalism have been stirred to their depths, that there has been a great searching of hearts and a great quickening of religious feeling. It looks as if with the Requiem Masses for the dead, there is united, as if by common consent, a general union of prayer for Ireland amounting almost to exaltation.

The *Bulletin* was instrumental in moulding this mood of exaltation, as well as recording it. The July issue sold out in a week. Censorship under the Defence of the Realm Act (DORA) meant that overt pro-Rising opinion published in newspapers was banned, and presses could be confiscated. Narratives by insurgents could not yet be published in Ireland, though several collections of articles and essays were brought out in America. The *Bulletin* evaded censorship but kept the Rising in the forefront of the public mind by publishing laudatory obituaries of the leaders every month. The model was that of the Lives of the Saints. Stories were told of their upright characters, their devout Catholicism, their courage and their care for others, all accompanied by photographs and drawings. The hagiographical sketches brought home to readers

– who could buy the *Bulletin* without embarrassment after Mass – that the rebels were not German stooges but Irishmen and Catholics, who had devoted themselves to their nation.

The socialist Connolly was rehabilitated as a devout man who had prayed for those who shot him: 'A man of great intellectual attainments, undoubted military genius and quite exceptional gifts of oratory, he unselfishly gave his whole adult life to the amelioration of the lot of his fellow workers. Many beautiful things could be written of his last days and of his glorious, if tragic, death.' The story of Michael Mallin's death was 'as fascinating as a romance and as grand as an epic'. His last letter to his wife revealed his devotion to God:

> O Saviour of man, if my dear ones could enter heaven with me how blessed and happy I would be; they would be away from the cares and trials of the world. Una, my little one, be a nun, Joseph, my little man, be a priest if you can. James and John to you the care of your mother, Make yourselves good strong men for her sake, and remember Ireland.

The story of Casement focused on his conversion to Catholicism and deathbed prayers. Sheehy Skeffington apparently died with a smile on his lips. Leaders and men alike died with Christian courage and humility, offering enlightenment to those left behind: 'it was edifying to witness the devotion with which he used to kiss the crucifix and repeat little ejaculatory prayers. Though in the greatest pain, he was most patient, and bore all with noble Christian fortitude.' Mass cards were printed with halos round the heads of the leaders.

These hagiographical sketches were leavened with mystical pieces such as 'A Mother's Vigil' by Mairead Ní Cuinneagháin, which told the tale of a black robed figure wending her way out of the city to the 'national cemetery':

> Side by side they lie, clasped close to the breast of the motherland they loved and served so well. Close by, the spirit of the Nation keeps vigil over their graves. Protectingly she hovers near them. Around them all, Eire draws her mantle of fresh, verdant shamrocks, fragrant with the dew resting lightly upon them. Overhead the rustling leaves continually breathe a low requiem in tender remembrance of their fate ... Like the true mother that she is, Eire guards them well. To the lonely watcher she whispers softly that their sacrifices have not been in vain. Their life blood shall rejuvenate and replenish the living spring of Ireland's hopes and Ireland's national aspirations. Sheltered within her loving arms they slumber peacefully, knowing well their memories and their deeds will be recorded for evermore in the hearts of the Irish race. And, in hallowed sod they yet shall sleep, where a grateful nation one day shall raise a lasting tribute to their memory.

As the Catholic Church retrospectively recast itself as a rebel Church, the iconography of the Blessed Virgin Mary merged with that of Kathleen ni Houlihan, the mythical figure of Ireland, who demanded sacrifice of her sons that the nation might be free, and who was made famous in Yeats's play *Cathleen ni Houlihan*. The first production of the play at the Abbey in 1893, when 'Cathleen' was played by Maud Gonne, caused a sensation and gave rise to Yeats's later rhetorical lines, 'Did that play of mine send out/Certain men the English shot?'

The editor of the *Bulletin* rationalised the beatification of the rebels on the grounds that they were being traduced elsewhere. 'To prevent the scales of history from being weighed too heavily against them, the *Catholic Bulletin* has been able to put before its readers for the past twelve months the simple record of their lives ... placing in its true perspective the lives and the methods and the motives of the men of Easter Week.' In fact, by this point in 1917 his paper was pushing an open door, as Sinn Féin propaganda, election manifestos, radical publications and Rising memorabilia kept the spotlight on the dead leaders.

It was the case, however, that in the immediate aftermath of the Rising detailed analysis of the battle was weighted against the rebels. Pro-British observers and participants had no difficulty in publishing their accounts in the mainstream press and in book form – there were no problems of censorship. London magazines such as *Blackwood's* and *St Martin's-le-Grand* published gory accounts of the behaviour of the rebels, and the difficulties faced by loyal citizens. The *Irish Times'* 'Sinn Fein Rebellion Handbook' included the text of the Royal Commission on the rebellion, copies of newspaper reports, lists of businesses damaged and individuals shot. Despite its anti-republican political stance it was immensely popular, feeding a public hungry for any information on what they had lived through. There were journalistic and quasi-historical accounts such as Wells and Marlowe's, *A History of the Irish Rebellion*, and *Six Days of the Irish Republic*, by a nephew of John Redmond, L. G. Redmond Howard, both of which came out in 1916. Even if these authors were partly sympathetic to the rebels, and attempted to be even-handed,

13. Walter Paget's famous painting, Scene in the General Post Office just before its evacuation *also known as* The Birth of the Republic. *The group in the foreground includes Connolly on a stretcher, his secretary Winny Carney offering him a drink, McDonagh crouching to take a message, and Plunkett in slouch hat with a scarf and crossed arms. Behind Plunkett Clarke looks directly at the viewer. Pearse is in profile, looking away from the messenger.*

there were no written accounts from the perspective of the insurgents to help them.

Part of the problem for the pro-rebel side was that the majority of their informants were in prison. But many of the women had not been held, and others were released early. In April 1917 the *Catholic Bulletin* began a series of accounts of the military actions. The series began with the events inside the GPO, and the story of the evacuation and surrender, told by Elizabeth O'Farrell and Julia Grennan. It was the beginning of a first-anniversary glut. The hazy symbolism of sword, righteous flame and Mother Ireland went along with attempts to reconstruct the minute details of the events of the week as newspapers tried to cater for their readers'

insatiable appetite for eyewitness accounts. Maps of engage-
ments were reproduced next to hagiographical portraits of
individual insurgents, emphasising their devotion to God
and the Irish nation.

The most potent of these early responses to the Rising
were those that blended the heroic and the realistic. Walter
Paget's painting 'Scene in the GPO just before its evacuation' was exemplary in this regard. The Press Censor saw
the propaganda value of the piece immediately, arguing that
publication would be 'inexpedient': 'It is an artistic production, very well grouped and designed, and would probably
become popular and help to spread sedition over Ireland.
After some years, it might be allowed to become part of
"history", when circumstances have changed.'

The painting shows the rebels meeting a desperate situation with fortitude. The GPO is on fire and the British are
closing in. No one panics. Each works at his allotted task,
including the priest whose blessing of the wounded insurgent casts a confessional glow over the whole scene. The
composition fuses action (the men firing at the windows)
and suffering (the *pietà*-like Connolly on his stretcher). It
handily includes portraits of all the leaders. Most of all it
infuses the detail of these last moments (the Volunteer uniforms; the GPO pillars) with mystical purpose. Take the
faraway resolute stare of Pearse – he is not looking at the
messenger but at destiny.

Alongside writing up their experiences for the first anniversary of the Rising the women of Cumann na mBan had
also been busy reconstructing an exact copy of the Proclamation of the Republic. The search for accuracy even extended
to using the same type as used for the original document,
which had somehow survived the bombardment of Liberty

14. *The elements of Paget's painting are reworked in this impression of the scene before the evacuation, published in* Our Boys, *the Christian Brother's magazine founded to compete with the British Boys Own genre. Connolly, Pearse and Clarke are among those in the foreground; the interior of the public office is signalled by the double pillars, arched windows (without sandbags) and glass roof.*

Hall. On Easter Monday morning, copies of the Proclamation were posted throughout the city on walls, letterboxes and election standards. Underneath the text of the Proclamation the message was blazoned in large type: 'The Irish Republic Still Lives'. The police went round the city scraping them off.

The events planned for this first anniversary were as much about re-enacting or continuing the Rising as commemorating it. It was clear from the start that the Rising reconstruction would take place at Easter (which fell two weeks earlier in 1917) rather than on 24 April. Unlike later commemorations, which were shifted to Easter Sunday, this first one was scheduled for the Monday – perhaps the identification of the rebels with the risen Christ was not yet secure. In the expectation of trouble, all processions and meetings were forbidden between Good Friday, 8 April, and the 15th. It was a cold Easter. During Sunday night, as it snowed, a republican flag was placed in position for hoisting the next day on the ruins of the GPO. The flag had been rolled but the wind caught it and by morning the three colours could be seen from the street. A large crowd began to gather. By noon it had grown to 'thousands'.

> Promptly at one o'clock – twelve old time – a young man was seen to move along slowly on the narrow ledge of the wall one hundred feet above the ground with little grip for his hands and less hold for his feet. He made his way to the corner and hoisted the flag amidst resounding cheers. At the same moment another Republican flag was floated atop of Nelson's Pillar and that too was loudly cheered. By 2pm police put the number at the GPO at 20,000. There was loud cheering at intervals and Republican badges, rosettes and armlets were generally worn. At a quarter to three a police constable sent up to take down the flag off the GPO was unable to do so without removing the pole. This he sawed through and it fell in the street where police and young men both dashed to capture it. The young men secured it amidst cheers and made off pursued by the police who failed to capture the flag.

These young men, and the women of Cumann na mBan, had the task of 'keeping the flame alive' – a task they executed on this occasion by stone throwing. The police responded with baton charges. The Rising was commemorated in a riot.

In July 1917 the release of convicted prisoners was celebrated with a literal flame, as fires were lit inside the ruins
of the GPO. This salute was for the living, but at its heart lay
what was fast becoming a cult of the dead. The ghosts of the
dead leaders, as W. B. Yeats pointed out, remained a palpa-
ble presence in the social landscape. In 'Sixteen Dead Men'
he suggested that the sacrificial logic of the dead lay counter
to the 'give and take' of diplomacy or the logic of politics.
Whatever one might think of the Rising, the dead leaders
were an inescapable part of the future for Ireland. The executions had made sure of that:

> O but we talked at large before
> The sixteen men were shot,
> But who can talk of give and take,
> What should be and what should not
> While those dead men are loitering there
> To stir the boiling pot?
>
> You say that we should still the land
> Till Germany's overcome;
> But who is there to argue that
> Now Pearse is deaf and dumb?
> And is their logic to outweigh
> MacDonagh's bony thumb?

⌛

April 1917 also saw the private circulation of W. B. Yeats's
poem 'Easter 1916', in an edition of twenty-five copies
printed by Clement Shorter. It is without doubt the most
famous literary response to the Rising. Written at Maud

Gonne's house in Normandy and Lady Gregory's at Coole during the spring and summer of 1916, the poem explores Yeats's own uncomfortable response to the Rising, which he experienced mostly at a distance. The poem traces the sudden transformation of the world of 'motley' and 'casual comedy' to the tragic certainties of rebel 'hearts with one purpose alone'. Yeats does allow his poem to do the work of elegy: 'I write it out in a verse – MacDonagh and Mac-Bride/And Connolly and Pearse'. And not only does he 'number' them in his song, he uses numbers to allude to the transformative date of the Rising. The poem consists of four stanzas, alternating between sixteen and twenty-four lines: 24/4/16. Yet 'Easter 1916' is an equivocal commemoration. Yeats acknowledges the radical force of the ideals that could lead men out to insurrection and likely death, yet he worries about the cost of such idealism to human integrity: 'what if excess of love/Bewildered them til they died?'

Yeats's famous poetic refrain, 'All's changed, changed utterly/A terrible beauty is born', was apparently suggested to him by a phrase in a letter from Maud Gonne: 'tragic dignity has returned to Ireland'. Perhaps not surprisingly, the poem did not satisfy Gonne's need for a powerful comment on the events. Her dislike of the poem grew partly from her own involvement in the Rising: her estranged husband Major John MacBride was one of the executed leaders, which put her in the company of the widows of the martyrs. Responding to Yeats's lines 'Too long a sacrifice/Can make a stone of the heart', she retorted that you 'know quite well that sacrifice has never yet turned a heart to stone though it has immortalised many & through it alone mankind can rise to God'.

In poems such as 'Easter 1916' and 'Sixteen Dead Men'

Yeats did articulate a strong sense of the changed political realities in Ireland after the Rising – the new force which had entered social and political life. Yet, as Maud Gonne knew, these poems also record his fascination with the tensions between doubt and certainty in his own mind. They are self-reflections, as well as reflections on the impact of the Rising. Nonetheless, they have to some extent been responsible for the popular belief that the Rising put an end to the give and take of thought, that everything was changed utterly in an instant. In reality, of course, the shifts in the popular understanding of the Rising were gradual, if fast. Political debate did not stop with the executions, as the discussions in Parliament, in newspapers and in socialist and pacifist circles attests. The 'martyrology' of the dead leaders was certainly a strong element within the cultural and social life of the nation, and this helped transform the fortunes of the Irish Parliamentary Party and moderate nationalism as a whole. Yet it was political events, such as the attempt by the British government to introduce conscription in Ireland in 1918, which ensured that the revolutionary politics of Sinn Féin would decisively defeat Home Rule in the general election that year.

Yeats was not the only writer to ask the question 'was it needless death after all?' There were straightforwardly critical works, such as St John Ervine's *Changing Winds*, or Eimear O'Duffy's *The Wasted Island*, which suggested that the Rising had been a mistake, destroying the hopes for Home Rule and bringing a cycle of violence in its wake. There were others which implied that the fault lay not with the insurgents, but with the community that refused to support them. Brinsley MacNamara wrote his second novel *The Clanking of Chains* in 1919. MacNamara had made his name with a controversial first novel that poured scorn on the crushing conservatism of the aspiring middle classes of small-town Ireland (the book was publicly burnt). *The Clanking of Chains* continued the theme, with a direct reference in the first pages to Yeats's death of Romantic Ireland. The townsfolk of Ballycullen 'fumble for their halfpence in the greasy tills', and come down hard on anyone with aspirations, such as Michael Dempsey, a shop assistant with 'the face and figure of an idealist'. The novel begins with Dempsey playing the part of Robert Emmet in a local drama production, but revolutionary idealism has a hard time of it in petit bourgeois Ballycullen. During Easter week the shopkeepers worry about the effect of the Rising on the banks and transfer their money from the Post Office to the barracks. Dempsey's dream of getting to the GPO is gently deflected by his girlfriend. 'In a day or two you'll be seeing how foolish all this wild adventure in Dublin was, and then, maybe, it's what you'll be thanking me.' A few months later, with GPO service now sanctified, she reproaches him for not having made the effort.

Who did or didn't get to the GPO and why was a frequent theme in the literature of the period, as idealism ran up against realism in the form of money, women, social conformism or simply personal fear. Maurice Dalton's 1918 play, *Sable and Gold*, was set in the drawing room of a comfortable middle-class family in Cork. News of the Rising comes and the young people of the household try to keep their parents from knowledge of the events. The twist in this play is that the mother (a Kathleen ni Houlihan figure) insists on bravery and the need for idealism. She does not want to be ashamed of her son. The father, who has been revealed as someone who does not understand the young, rejects this cult of sacrifice. At the end of the play their son Gerald returns home. He has run away from the GPO but cannot admit this to his mother. Encouraged by his sister, whose fiancé has been killed in the GPO, he decides to live a lie, embroidering for his mother a myth of glorious deeds.

Needless death, the corruption of ideals, the failure of heroism: novelistic treatments of the Rising tended to eschew a hagiographical tone, not least because they needed to set events in the context of a community, the family or the small town. Moreover the literary novelists had never been part of the revolutionary aesthetic project of the cultural revival. It was to poetry that most people looked for a fitting literary tribute to the Rising. What Yeats had referred to as 'writing it out in a verse' was a hugely popular way of responding to the Rising. Indeed the aesthetic response to events was very often a first response, suggesting that writing about what had happened was understood as efficacious in itself. In this the Rising poets were schooled by the huge corpus of poetry commemorating the soldiers of the First World War. And luckily for Maud Gonne, most poetic responses to the Rising embraced the nobility of the rebels' sacrifice far more wholeheartedly.

Poems, ballads and commemorative songs appeared in all sorts of publications, from local newspapers, to the radical political press, to ballad sheets selling on the streets of the city. Posthumous editions of the works of Pearse, Plunkett and MacDonagh were published throughout the latter half of 1916 and 1917. Pearse had apparently joked that should the Rising fail it would at least get rid of several bad poets, but in fact it raised their profile, and spawned many imitators. There were commemorative poems by a raft of middling poets associated with the rebels, such as

Joseph Campbell, Padraic Colum, Father Padraig de Brun, Dorothy Macardle, Alice Milligan and Ella Young. Many of the more substantial publications faced problems of censorship under the Defence of the Realm Act. Dermot O'Byrne (otherwise known as the English composer Arnold Bax) penned 'A Dublin Ballad', which was printed in 1918 by Colm O'Lochlainn but promptly banned. The Gaelic Press brought out a collection entitled *Aftermath* late in 1916. Poet, editor and printer were anonymous, though booksellers and newsagents could still be prosecuted for stocking it.

Most of these works peddled a mixture of Celtic Twilight mysticism, Catholic devotion, rebel ballad, and a form of Christian political symbolism that had strange echoes of the Salvation Army. The poems were full of images and symbols of dream, dawn, swift avenging flames, sacrifice, hope, resurrection and Kathleen ni Houlihan. Dora Sigerson Shorter, who was reputed (on her own admission) to have sickened and died of grief for Ireland in 1918, brought all these together in the poems published in her posthumous collection *The Tricolour*, as this representative snippet shows:

> They lit a fire within their land that long was ashes
>   cold.
> With splendid dreams they made it glow, threw in
>   their hearts of gold.
> They saw thy slowly paling cheek and knew thy
>   failing breath,
> They bade thee live once more, Kathleen, who was so
>   nigh to death.

Bravery and idealism were the staple fare of these poems, which set out to be elegiac and consolatory, and which are very difficult to take seriously from a contemporary perspective, steeped as we are in the language of disillusion and waste made famous by Owen and Sassoon. The style was easily recognisable, however, to those familiar with the mass of popular English war poetry. Poetry was virtually a mass medium in wartime Britain. Far more well known than the mould-breaking works of intellectuals in the trenches, consoling war poetry was published everywhere in newspapers, written privately by civilians, incorporated in letters home. Several Irish poets, such as Katherine Tynan, wrote elegiac pro-war verse which was hugely popular in Britain. The bulk of this poetry speaks through the inherited idioms of nineteenth-century verse, fusing patriotism and English pastoral with Victorian values of honour, chivalry and sacrifice. Irish 'Rising verse' shares with its English counterpart a preoccupation with Christian sacrifice, which is recast as Imperial sacrifice in a great deal of First World War literature. Conflating Christ the martyr with the war dead helped justify mass slaughter; the army was cast as a missionary force fighting to save souls. In the work of Robert Bridges or Rupert Brooke, for example, readers entered the world of the soldier-poet-hero, where the language of resurrection was never far away.

One aspect of English war poetry that didn't cross over into Rising verse was the elegiac pastoral. Though some Irish war poets such as Francis Ledwidge did try incorporating English pastoral into their poetry (remembering County Meath and 'the little fields/That call across the world to me'), for the most part corners of foreign fields, like medieval chivalry, were dispensed with, and in their place fragments of a would-be Irish idiom were introduced: Gaelic romanticism; Celtic legend; internal rhyme; the styles and techniques of the Irish Literary Revival. But what is most striking about Rising verse is the sheer volume of it. One Dublin priest wrote to a colleague in the Vatican in the summer of 1916: 'The number of MS poems in circulation is amazing – mostly very good. The latest I saw is one "Shall Casement die?", a fine but perfervid protest as to what will happen if the inconceivable takes place.'

Irish poets and versifiers suddenly had fifteen dead leaders to elegise. By August, when Casement was hanged as a traitor in London, there would be sixteen. Many of the leaders had been writers, and were thus 'owed' a written tribute. One difficulty posed by the simultaneous deaths of so many leaders was how to differentiate them in poetry. There is, for example, nothing particularly reminiscent of Plunkett in the poem dedicated to his memory by the American Catholic convert Joyce Kilmer, though the challenge to Yeats is signalled in technicolour:

'Romantic Ireland's dead and gone,
It's with O'Leary in the grave.'
Then, Yeats, what gave that Easter dawn
A hue so radiantly brave?
There was a rain of blood that day,
Red rain in gay blue April weather.
It blessed the earth till it gave birth
To valour thick as blooms of heather.

Then there was the homage to be paid to the prisoners. Traditional elegiac responses became overloaded, but for the most part the poets did not find a new way of going about it. They stuck to a Catholic version of Georgian romanticism (the image of the rose was indispensable to popular sentimental texts of the war, just as much as of the Rising), spiced up with Celtic symbols.

The radical 'mosquito' press began printing again in Dublin in June 1916. Alongside articles designed to keep the Rising uppermost in everyone's minds, and to harness the growing anti-British feeling to Sinn Féin, these small political papers printed reams of Rising poetry rivalling the reams of similarly indifferent trench verse. *Irish Opinion*, for example, published some of the leading lights of the Gaelic League (those who weren't dead or in prison), such as T. F. O'Rahilly, M. J. Macmanus, Thomas Shaw, Maurice Dalton, Austin Clarke and Grace Plunkett (her 'To the Leaders' published in October 1916 comforted its readers by reminding them that 'God did not die in vain on Calvary'). Liberally scattered with 'Swords outleaping the dark eyes of Erin' and the 'wounded lips' of Kathleen ni Houlihan, these poems, amounting to five or six per issue, in Irish and English, were attempts at an Irish style. There were also rather odder verses, such as 'Ode to Algy', by 'Maud', which was described in *The Irish Nation* as having been 'Found in the Trenches':

> O nut, scarce ripe, but full of youthful promise,
> What dire chance placed you in command of
>   Tommies?
> What wizard caused your spatted feet to roam
> So far from Grafton Street, their proper home?

Dillon's speech to the Commons in May 1916 had compared the men fighting in Ireland with those on the Continent. The stress on valour emphasised the soldierly nature of the rebels, pairing them with the soldiers on the Western Front. But there were other points of comparison, such as that both rebels and wartime volunteers were 'scarce ripe'. Early Sinn Féin propaganda had tried mockery of Redmond's Volunteers, but, particularly after the catastrophe at Suvla Bay – continually brought to mind by the scores of wounded now back in Ireland – the general attitude of nationalists was less anger than pity. In the months before the Rising, Irish anti-war propaganda had been full of the idea that Redmond's Volunteers were 'misguided'. In February 1916 Connolly had been lamenting those 'poor misguided brothers of ours', who had been 'tricked and deluded into giving battle for England'. This line acknowledged the courage of Irishmen in action while the leaders (and recruiters) could still be roundly condemned as cowards and hypocrites.

The term 'misguided' was one that the Irish Parliamentary Party would fling back at the rebels with a vengeance. The suggestion in early responses to the Rising that the rank and file of the rebels were 'dupes' of the leaders mirrored advanced nationalist propaganda, but this distinction between honest volunteer and traitorous leader was harder to maintain after the leaders had been executed. When Irish Parliamentarists Tom Kettle (Sheehy Skeffington's brother-in-law) and Willie Redmond (John Redmond's brother) were killed in action in France, they too became idealists rather than cynical politicians. The poet George Russell (otherwise known as AE), friend of Yeats, made the comparison explicit in his poem 'Salutation' by interweaving elegiac stanzas about those who had died in Dublin, including Sheehy Skeffington, with those who had died in France, including Tom Kettle and Francis Ledwidge. Ledwidge himself had enlisted reluctantly, initially siding with the separatist Irish Volunteers rather than Redmond's men in 1914. Posted to Gallipoli in 1915 he was on sick leave at home in Meath when the Rising took place and as the executions and round-ups continued he reacted by turning to drink; he reported late for duty and was court-martialled for insulting superior officers. Ledwidge's most famous poem is his elegy for his friend Thomas MacDonagh, and his own story clearly reveals the complex motives of Irishmen fighting on the British side. Nonetheless, the equivalence in AE's poem was too much for some people. When it was republished in a twentieth-anniversary collection of 1916 poetry, the editor chose the earlier version, which omitted all the stanzas elegising the men who died in the trenches – an act in itself revealing the gradual shift away from acknowledging Irish First World War soldiers, an 'amnesia' which became entrenched during the Second World War.

Over the next few years, awareness of the kinship between those fighting in Dublin and those in the Great War was travestied by numerous point-scoring exercises on both sides. One of the most egregious is surely Canon Charles O'Neil's 1919 song 'The Foggy Dew', with its sickeningly self-satisfied line that it's 'better to die 'neath an Irish sky than at Suvla or Sud el Bar'. The line was echoed, though with more sympathy, in 'Gallipoli': 'All those fine young men who marched to foreign shores/To fight the wars when the greatest war of all was at home.'

For all the comparisons between the soldiers in the trenches and the Volunteers in the GPO, however, and for all the stylistic echoes between First World War and Rising verse, the differences were vast. There was first of all the massive difference in scale – beyond individual elegy any comparison between the Volunteers in Dublin and the soldiers at the Front involved an almost obscene form of magnification, given the scale of the losses. First World War poetry had to confront the problem of how to express near universal grief; it was engaged in a search for meaning that was as much existential as artistic or political. Rising verse utilised some of the conventions of this social form of mourning, but in order to claim political (and artistic) legitimacy. The greatest difference between the poets of the First World War and of the Rising was that the Rising poets saw themselves as continuing the revolutionary cultural project begun by the dead leaders. Pearse, Plunkett and MacDonagh had formed a self-conscious artistic elite whose works, including the Rising, were to wake Ireland to a consciousness of itself. Their aesthetic and political ideals were of a piece. Much of the commemorative Rising verse needs to be understood as continuing that revolutionary political project.

The compulsive repetition of images of the rebels' idealism and otherworldliness was in part a response to the language in which the Rising had been couched. Symbols of hope, dream and mystical regeneration were perhaps necessarily vague before the Rising itself, and certainly before any clear plan of campaign had been formulated. Who could challenge Pearse's rhetorical question:

> O wise men riddle me this: what if the dream come
>   true?
> What if the dream come true, and if millions unborn
>   shall dwell
> In the house that I shaped in my heart, the noble
>   house of my thought?

Now that the Rising had happened, however, it wasn't entirely clear what had come to pass. Mystical, symbolic and religious images were one way of approaching an event that still seemed hard to comprehend, and of gesturing to its revolutionary potential.

The best example of a literary work attempting revolutionary transformation is not a poem but Daniel Corkery's short play 'Resurrection', written in 1918 but promptly banned from publication. The rebellion has broken out in Dublin and the audience watch the impact of events on a family farm some miles out of the city. Terence, the old farmer, was out in the Fenian Rising of 1867 but is now financially comfortable and fearful of losing the land and position he has gained. His younger son, Shawn, supports the rebels but tries to keep from his father the news that his brother Michael is in the Rising. As Terence insists that all talk of revolution now is mere foolishness, news comes that Michael is being sent back from Dublin in the middle of the night. Terence becomes terrified that Michael has betrayed his colleagues: 'What's bringing him, do ye know? Is he bringing news of the rising or what? My God. He's running away! He's after deserting them – his comrades.' The fear that his son is a traitor to the cause rouses Terence out of his complacency. When it becomes clear that Michael is retuning home because he has been mortally wounded, Terence gives his blessing to Shawn to join the revolt: 'go out to the fight, Shawn, like the men of old.'

The crux of the play is that the young generation must once more teach the old the necessity for sacrifice. What looks like foolishness is the catalyst for national resurrection. Michael's death, probably Shawn's too, will rejuvenate the moribund society, which has forgotten the value of ideals. The greatest fear is not of death but of cowardice.

The play is almost embarrassingly simple propaganda. Corkery sets up an opposition between the complacency and conformity of the older generation (for which read the Irish Parliamentary Party and Home Rule), and the dignity of youthful rebellion, which brings spiritual regeneration even when doomed to failure. It is a play about the power of the will to bring about cultural transformation, a rewriting of Kathleen ni Houlihan to take account of the Rising, and it is the kind of thing Yeats must have had in mind when he imagined MacDonagh's bony thumb, or the right rose tree watered by the blood of Pearse and Connolly.

Right up until the civil war, and indeed beyond, popular poetry and religious rhetoric took on the task of idealising the rebels and keeping them in mind. Realist 'documentary' accounts tended to be infused with a similar heroic diction. Within little more than a year of the Rising, through a combination of arguments about British militarism, the religious rhetoric of martyrdom, the effects of the executions and the idealism of the revolutionary project, debates about the Rising had narrowed to a stark opposition between realism (or conformity) and idealism (or fanaticism). This was to dominate discussion of the Rising for most of the century that followed.

4

COMMEMORATION

They shall be spoken of among their people
The generations shall remember them
And call them blessed.

Patrick Pearse, 'The Mother' (1916)

The new O'Connell Street seems to me to hold now all that
is most modern of Irish life. There are cinemas with restau-
rants and ballrooms attached, and cafés, and the young men
and women who throng them might belong to any continen-
tal city. At evening, when the illuminated signs flash across
the streets or over the river, and the pavements are crowded,
one does not recognise the Dublin one knew.

Pamela Hinkson, *The Light on Ireland* (1935)

In the twilight years of the British administration in Ireland, the ruined GPO acted above all as a reminder that the revolution was unfinished. What was at stake in invocations of the GPO was not so much the commemoration of the Rising, as its continuation. Each year the inheritors of the Rising – reborn as the Irish Republican Army – sought out more imaginative ways of letting the British know it wasn't over yet. At Easter 1920, with the War of Independence at its most intense, British soldiers built barbed-wire entanglements around Dublin in order to prevent a second, 'anniversary' Rising. But rather than target the city's revolutionary landmarks the IRA burnt out tax offices and barracks throughout the country, in a series of punctually co-ordinated Easter fires designed to be at once commemorative and a sign of the still-revolutionary present. They were announcing their unbroken allegiance to the independent Republic proclaimed outside the GPO in 1916 and reminding the world that the national struggle would continue as long as the British remained in Ireland.

The passing of the Anglo-Irish Treaty in 1922 brought the War of Independence to an end. The Act established the Irish Free State as an autonomous dominion of the British Empire, and provided an opt-out clause for Northern Ireland. With the founding of the Free State the symbolism of the GPO changed utterly. It became at one stroke a source of political legitimacy, and a focus for internal dissent.

Power now lay in the hands of former revolutionaries, and the Rising, which was already part of national mythology, became respectable. Whereas a few years before, poems invoking 1916 were circulated in samizdat fashion and you could be arrested for wearing a Sinn Féin badge or singing 'Who Fears to Speak of Easter Week', now suddenly the GPO stood as the foundation of the new polity. Volunteers – those in favour of the Anglo-Irish Treaty, who were to be on the winning side in the civil war – put aside their gunman roles and took up posts in the civil administration, in the army or in the police force. As the historian F. X. Martin put it much later:

Many of the brave men, who had turned out in 1916 with rifles but unable to afford a uniform, now appeared resplendent in military attire or as ministers of state and high-ranking officials in morning suits and top hats. It became apparent that they were not blood-thirsty or anarchical but were hard-working, earnest, and determined to translate the revolution into a day-to-day administration of government. One had to accept that Pearse and the revolutionaries were right, or at least that they had been successful.

But the difference between being right and being successful was still impossibly broad for those republicans who refused to accept the terms of the Anglo-Irish Treaty, with its oath of allegiance to the British Crown and – the issue that would later come to dominate Anglo-Irish politics throughout the twentieth century – partition between north and south. Pearse may have been right, but according to these irreconcilables he hadn't yet been successful, and those who took power in the new state were usurping the authority of the true Republic. The GPO and the ideals of the Proclamation had been betrayed. In the agonising debates over whether to accept the treaty in January 1922, the Republic proclaimed outside the GPO in 1916 was invoked by both sides. To those who argued that Pearse would have accepted the terms offered by the British, their opponents insisted the reverse was true. Margaret Pearse, the bereaved mother, stood up to claim that 'the ghosts of my sons would haunt me' if she were to vote in favour of the treaty: 'Remember, the day will come – soon I hope, Free State or otherwise – when those bones shall be lifted as if they were the bones of saints.' Harry Boland, a veteran of the GPO, invoked the 'stainless' tradition of Irish republicanism that had been handed down through the generations, insisting there

15. A photograph, almost certainly posed, taken during the civil war. The image shows Free State troops taking aim against republican forces at O'Connell Bridge in July 1922. The republican poster claims continuity between the present IRA struggle and the Rising, with the headline 'Easter Week Repeats Itself – The IRA Still Defends The Republic'.

should be no compromise. 'If we are prepared to carry on this fight the people will support us.' Fight on they did, but against themselves.

The failure to reach agreement on the treaty precipitated a bloody and divisive civil war. For years afterwards, opponents in that war were unable to be in the same room as one another. Government ministers had ordered the arrest and execution of old friends; the IRA had murdered former comrades in reprisal. In 1924, a year after the civil war ended, the first formal military ceremony to commemorate the Rising took place at Arbour Hill, since the GPO was still a ruin. It was a one-sided affair. Invitations were sent out by the Cumann na Gaedheal government (the first formal government of the Free State formed in 1923 from the pro-treaty wing of Sinn Féin) to participants and relatives across the political spectrum, but only Michael Mallin's widow accepted. In 1926 the tenth-anniversary tribute fell decidedly flat as only government supporters turned up. Rival commemorations were held by anti-treaty republicans at the Republican burial plot in Glasnevin, setting in motion a yearly back-and-forth over the timings of parades, in an effort to ensure that no two politically opposed commemorations turned up at any of the crucial sites at the same moment.

In this bitter atmosphere of accusation and counter-accusation the Rising dominated the political landscape. Deputies were chosen as much for their national record as their political skills. This was inevitable, given the public pillorying of those who had not had the opportunity to be 'out' in 1916, or – worse – had not taken the opportunity. The taunting of political opponents with versions of 'Where were you in 1916?' was so well honed it became a national joke. As split followed split in the republican movement, former revolutionary allies who were now sworn enemies took to dropping vicious little asides about each other's readiness to sacrifice all for the nation. So, for example, Tom Clarke's widow Kathleen Clarke noted acerbically in her memoir how Sean T. O'Kelly (then Minister for Finance in the wartime Fianna Fáil government) brought her a message on the Thursday of Easter week and stayed for a leisurely cup of tea. He 'didn't seem in a hurry' to get back.

Judging the new state's politicians on their revolutionary record was undoubtedly backward-looking. As Cumann na Gaedheal TD Gearoid O'Sullivan put it during one particularly acrimonious debate in the Dáil, 'We all know where we were then and what we want to know is where we are now.' Since he had actually been in the GPO (and had raised the flag on the building at the beginning of Easter week) he could perhaps afford to be cavalier. Nonetheless, 1916 was a ticket to political power, not only for those who fought but for their relations, such as Patrick and Willie Pearse's mother and Thomas Clarke's wife. For the wives and mothers of dead leaders, political status clearly derived from their proximity to sacrifice. They had surrendered their menfolk, after all. But for the majority of TDs the relationship with 1916 was rather more awkward. Yes, many of them had risked their lives, some had been under death sentences, most had been imprisoned for a time. But even as they made their rhetorical gestures to the men of 1916 in the Dáil, it was clear that these particular rebels had done very well out of the Rising. This only made the debt to be paid to their dead comrades all the more acute. As Yeats had seen within a few months of the Rising, the living were from now on to be in hock to the ghosts of 1916: MacDonagh's bony thumb was also a pointing finger.

While the Free State government was scorned by republicans for selling out, it also had to hold the line against imperial tub-thumping by Unionists, for whom the very thought of the Republic declared in 1916 was anathema. The sacralisation of the GPO took place in a context in which commemorations were already highly politicised. In the North, for example, the Battle of the Somme was being revised as a symbol of loyalism. On Remembrance Day 1922 James Craig, Prime Minister of the newly formed Northern Irish state, asserted that 'those who passed away have left behind a great message to all of them to stand firm, and to give away none of Ulster's soil.' This loyalist message was relayed at

Remembrance services throughout the North as 11 November was remoulded as 12 July, echoing the cry of 'No surrender'. Five years later the Cumann na Gaedheal government had to deal with a petition to turn Merrion Square – directly outside the Houses of the Oireachtas, or Parliament – into a Great War memorial park. There was immediate concern that Remembrance Day parades, passing directly under the windows of the Dáil, would prove a focus for anti-government agitation. Moreover, as the Minister for Justice Kevin O'Higgins put it, the location of the memorial in Merrion Square, right next to the seat of government, would 'give a wrong twist, as it were, a wrong suggestion, to the origins of this State'. The visitor might 'conclude that the origins of this State were connected with that park and the memorial in that park, were connected with the lives that were lost in the Great War in France, Belgium, Gallipoli and so on. That is not the position.' (Within three months of this speech O'Higgins was to be murdered by three republicans in retaliation for the execution of IRA prisoners, one of whom had been best man at his wedding.)

The origins of the state resided instead in the burnt-out building on O'Connell Street. By 1926 the idea of noble sacrifice at the GPO was firmly established as a foundation stone of the new Irish polity. The physical reconstruction of the building lagged a good way behind. The British government had found work for demobbed soldiers in the immediate aftermath of the Great War in clearing the debris from O'Connell Street. But any repairs were destroyed again in 1922 and the area lay in ruins for years. In 1924 the Free State government unveiled plans for the refurbishment of the building, in grand Art Deco style, using the rental from new shopping arcades to defray the cost. The ambitious plans of the Greater Dublin Reconstruction Movement for a rational, planned and modern city centre went by the board. The frontispiece to 'Dublin of the Future', the prize-winning Dublin town plan by Patrick Abercrombie, was a haunting image by Harry Clarke. A gaunt and terrifying figure of death towers over the burning GPO, the Customs House and the Four Courts on the left of the picture; with his right hand he props up the crumbling tenements crowded with the poor. Abercrombie's design for a new city centre included bold proposals to clear away the slums and shift the focus from O'Connell Street. They were rejected by the government, which chose to keep both slums and GPO.

The restoration was dogged by delays (they were still clearing the site in 1926) and complaints that builders and contractors were not taking their national duty seriously enough – there were wrangles over using Portland rather than Irish stone, and optimistic suggestions that the building works could be used to solve the problem of unemployment. But the GPO was finally re-opened in 1929 by W. T. Cosgrave, Cumann na Gaedheal leader and one of the Volunteers who had been posted there in Easter week. In addition to the spacious new public office, all polished mahogany and brass, the Post Office boasted a large accounting section, a savings bank and, on the second floor, the state's ambitious new venture in broadcasting: radio studios, equipped with then state-of-the-art microphones and sound-proofing. The Department of Posts and Telegraphs was to become the largest arm of the Irish civil service, but the government was not shy about taking advantage of private commercial enterprise, funding the revamped building through rents from the retail outlets in the new glassed-in arcade and the shops in Henry Street.

16. In June 1929 William Cosgrave, leader of the Cumann na Gaedheal government, officially opened the restored Post Office with a silver key, which was presented to him as a memento of the occasion.

Commerce was to the fore at the opening ceremony, when Cosgrave applauded the restoration of the building as 'symbolical of the new order – and the Irish Nation is progressing on the path of prosperity'. Nonetheless, he looked a little uncertain as the cameras snapped this historic moment; admittedly it was rather a small key for such a big door.

Cosgrave may also have been conscious of the number of people in the new state he had failed to carry with him. The restoration of the GPO signalled the beginning of the building's life as a backdrop for independent Ireland's political theatre. From now on, political claims and counter-claims were to be increasingly focused through the building itself. In 1929 (as the Wall Street Crash loomed) Cosgrave wanted to project prosperity; later the building would be used by de Valera to project communal solidarity, and even military strength. In each case the trick was to harness the symbolism of the old revolutionary GPO to the changed circumstances of the modern nation. Indeed the decision to install the state radio station upstairs in the GPO (later to be joined by television) was a clear signal of the intention to mould the building in the shape of the modern nation, rather than the nation in the shape of the building. Yet these very public attempts, through speeches and commemorations, to make the GPO stand for the new Ireland also acted as reminders of the old.

As Cosgrave intoned the virtues of the modern prosperous nation in 1929, a group of republican women ran up a flyer extolling the incomparably greater virtues of 'The Old GPO', and the struggle it symbolised. Attacking Cosgrave as the 'traitor head of a usurping government', the poster stuck up on walls around the city asked:

Is there another country in the world where a man
    who had sold his country would be allowed to
    desecrate the memory of a national hero?
Has Pearse's sacrifice been in vain?

Has Clarke's heroic example of 14 long years in
   British dungeons followed by many years of
   preparation for 1916 all been forgotten?
Has the Conquest been completed? The Answer lies
   with YOU.
YOU have the power to overthrow the two usurping
   governments in Ireland and make it possible for
   the Irish Republic to function.
In 1916, that little band of 687 Volunteers held their
   own against the thousands of British Soldiers who
   were in first-class fighting form.
Is this generation less heroic than preceding
   generations? No.
We do not deserve to be free if we allow England's
   subordinates to hold our country in bondage.
Our opportunity may arise any day. Are you ready?
Join Ireland's Revolutionary Organisations.
Prepare for the great day. Let us [sic] our next war
   end in Victory.

Cumann na mBan's paean to the republican values of the
old GPO contained the seeds of a Rising riposte that over the
years was to rival and outstrip 'Where were you in 1916?':
the betrayal of the lost leaders. If Pearse and his comrades in
arms were to return to Ireland now, what would they think?
They would find emigration, unemployment, toadying to
Britain, but above all partition – a catalogue of horrors that
was to be recounted right through the twentieth century as
the sacrifice at the GPO was used to condemn the failures of
the modern state.
   This attack by those styling themselves the true heirs of
the Republic clearly echoed the terms in which the treaty

had initially been rejected – the fight for the Republic must continue. It was closely linked to a third accusation that was to mark GPO rivalry over the years. This was the explicit challenge to the current generation to live up to the ideals of the original Volunteers and to prepare for war. This invocation of generation was in itself a kind of commemoration of the Rising – the Proclamation had argued for the need for the generation of 1916 to prove itself as their rebel forefathers had done six times in the preceding 300 years. It is perhaps not surprising that this recurrent demand was central to GPO counter-demonstrations, as republicans urged the need to continue the war against Britain. But the appeal to the young generation to live up to the ideals of 1916 also became part of official Rising commemorations right through the middle years of the twentieth century, and particularly in 1966. This had less to do with fomenting war (though this would be the accusation thrown at the 1966 commemorations) than with encouraging the current generation not to ignore the Rising entirely. In another reprise of Pearsean rhetoric, the problem was that the national consciousness was moribund.

In the early years of the Free State, however, there seemed little danger of historical amnesia. Throughout the 1920s those for and against the treaty fought over the bones of the Rising, and the mixture of pious reverence and political point-scoring with which it was treated soon gave rise to a more general disillusion about the revolution as a whole.

By the time this cartoon was published in *Dublin Opinion* in 1924, the story of the GPO had passed decisively into the realm of myth, so much so that its legendary status was already the butt of jokes. The Rising was untouchable, but for that very reason it was targeted as a source of political corruption, as people vied with one another to claim

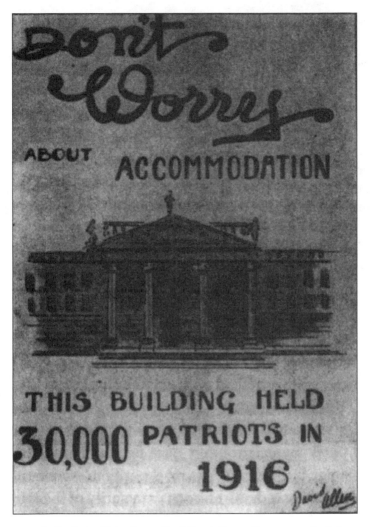

17. *In the immediate aftermath of the civil war the pressure to claim participation in the Rising was immense. This cartoon was published in the 'humorous journal'* Dublin Opinion *in August 1924. The portico appears to be drawn with steps, showing that the story that Pearse had read the Proclamation from the steps of the GPO was already firmly accepted, even though the building had no steps.*

association with it. The satirical bite in cartoons such as this was later to surface in a thriving sub-genre of Irish theatrical satire that took the commemoration of nationalist heroes as its target – political farces such as Louis MacNeice's 1935 *Station Bell* or Flann O'Brien's wartime play *Faustus Kelly*.

The most famous satire on 1916 is undoubtedly Sean O'Casey's play *The Plough and the Stars*, which was staged at the Abbey Theatre in 1926. By the mid 1920s O'Casey had already made a name for himself with plays about recent political events – *The Shadow of a Gunman* had addressed the impact of the War of Independence on working-class Dubliners; in *Juno and the Paycock* it was the civil war. In *The Plough and the Stars* O'Casey again focused on ordinary tenement dwellers caught up in political events, but the satirical and critical edge to his play was more than his audience could bear. On the fourth night there were riots in the theatre.

The actors were interrupted in the middle of Act 2. The scene is set in the inside of a pub in the autumn of 1915. Outside a political meeting is taking place; the audience see the back of the speaker's head through the window and hear snatches of his speech, which are easily recognisable as edited highlights from speeches by Pearse and Connolly:

> The old heart of the earth needs to be warmed with the red wine of the battlefields ... Such august homage was never offered to God as this: the homage of millions of lives given gladly for love of country. And we must be ready to pour out the same red wine in the same glorious sacrifice, for without suffering there is no redemption!

Inside the pub, and directly counterpointing the language of revolutionary blood-sacrifice, the scene reveals the less than edifying lives of the local residents. Women fight, a baby gets left on the floor, a prostitute looks for business, while men who have no ideals drunkenly praise the language of war. ('I was burnin' to dhraw me sword, an' wave an' wave it over me'). Much of this is pretty direct satire, but the last two acts of the play, which focus on the events of Easter week as seen from the perspective of non-participants, and primarily the women living in the tenement, move beyond satire. The chaotic scenes pile tragedy upon tragedy (at one point a coffin on stage holds two bodies) and in so doing empty the events of all tragic efficacy. A young girl dies of TB, a wife loses her baby and her mind, a woman is shot by mistake and dies cursing. Though some of the residents join the Rising, O'Casey implies that they do so not out of conviction but out of fear: 'I tell you they're afraid to say they're afraid!' In this relentless attack on the values of the Rising, death is not only without glory but without meaning. The violence brings looting, disunity and the death of nearly all the women in the play, but certainly no redemption.

The Plough and the Stars was not the first play to puncture the heroic aura surrounding the GPO – Maurice Dalton's coward rebel from Cork had done that; and novels as various as Ervine's *Changing Winds* (1917) and Eimear O'Duffy's *The Wasted Island* (1919) had condemned the Rising as a whole (a 'catastrophe', according to O'Duffy). But the audience for these works was tiny. Part of the reason *The Plough and the Stars* caused such a stir was the Abbey's reputation as a national institution. The protests against the play were planned rather than spontaneous, orchestrated by a number of women whose relatives had died in 1916, including Hanna Sheehy Skeffington, widow of Francis Sheehy Skeffington who was shot in Portobello Barracks. There was a sense of fury that the theatre which had put on Yeats's play *Cathleen ni Houlihan* was now holding up to 'derision and obloquy the men and women of Easter Week':

> In no country save in Ireland could a State-subsidised theatre presume on popular patience to the extent of making a mockery and a byword of a revolutionary movement on which the present structure claims to stand.

But there was far more at stake than the state subsidy. The riot crystallised for perhaps the first time the battle between first-hand experience and fictional (or historical) interpretation which was to centre on the events in the GPO. The play purported to show the Rising through the eyes of some who did not take part, and whose lives were blighted by it. But the audience included many who had taken part in the Rising, and who felt they knew what had happened. As Sheehy Skeffington put it, 'I am one of the widows of Easter Week. It is no wonder that you do not remember Easter Week because none of you fought on either side. The play is going to London to be advertised there because it belies Ireland.'

Insisting on their right to comment on O'Casey's portrait of the Rising, the protestors argued for interpretation by the people and for the people, rather than by a tiny group of intellectuals. 'The only censorship that is justified is the free censorship of popular opinion. The Ireland that remembers with tear-dimmed eyes all that Easter Week stands for, will not, and cannot, be silent in face of such a challenge.' The conflict between one playwright's interpretation and popular recall was thus set up as a conflict between realism and idealism, with the widows arguing forcefully for the

importance of idealism. O'Casey's decision to focus relent-
lessly on a hyper-real (indeed melodramatic) vision of the
squalor and hopelessness of tenement life meant that there
was no place to portray the inspiration (Sheehy Skeffington
used the word 'glory') that was also part of the events. *The
Plough and the Stars* recast Pearse's inspiring speeches as
fodder for the gossiping locals in the pub, and if anyone was
idealised in the play it was the looters.

In 1925 Liam O'Flaherty had published *The Informer*, a
gritty naturalist portrait of the effects of poverty on former
revolutionaries. Set in a very similar Dublin working-class
milieu, it is a book that targets head-on the yawning gap
between revolutionary ideals and the mundane reality
which began to dawn after 1922. As George Russell put it in
a review of the novel, 'If Cuchullain had not been so noble,
the Informer would not have been so ignoble.' Yet O'Flaherty
was one of those who objected to *The Plough and the Stars*,
and joined in the protests. For the play did not anatomise the
failure of the state, but attacked its very foundation, showing
the violence of the Rising to have been purely destructive,
and politics itself futile. O'Casey's attack on the Rising was
as much an attack on the myths that it fostered as on the
event itself. When the young wife Nora exclaims, 'My Jack
will be killed, my Jack will be killed! … He is to be butchered
as a sacrifice to th' dead!' it is clear that O'Casey had in mind
the dead of 1916 as much as Pearse's previous revolutionary
generations.

The conflict between realism and idealisation was to
become central to criticism of the Rising from the 1960s
onwards, when 'revisionist' historians began to call into
question some of the myths of the Rising in the name of
accurate historical analysis. O'Casey's play became hugely

popular at that time, since it seemed to offer an analysis of the 'real' lives of working-class Dubliners in contrast to Pearsean rhetoric. The rioters of 1926 were represented as clinging to myths in the face of O'Casey's realism, and statements about Irish tear-dimmed eyes seem to prove it.

But the protest was more subtle than that, cutting across the opposition between myth and fact. The idealism of the insurgents had also been part of the 'real' experience in Dublin in 1916, argued Hanna Sheehy Skeffington. Her point was that the play was in its own way just as partial as the reams of stories of noble sacrifice which were published to mark the tenth anniversary, as her son Owen Sheehy Skeffington recalled in a BBC interview forty years later:

> She didn't deny at all that what he said in the play was true, but she said, it's not the whole truth and these things are too close to us now, to have a play put on which is so one-sided. My own feeling at that time, and I argued it with her because I was, by that time, seventeen, was that O'Casey was not trying to show the rebellion, he was trying to show the impact of a revolution upon the submerged tenth, upon the person who is so oppressed by poverty and exploitation that he hasn't even enough sense to loot properly. He's the kind of person who can go out and come back with a pramful of umbrellas when he's looking for loot. And it seemed to me that O'Casey got across brilliantly the harrowing experience of slumdom and that it – that the rebellion, in a sense – was only incidental to it.

The business over *The Plough and the Stars* proved costly for O'Casey, who never lived in Ireland again, but one thing it showed was that – for all the bitter civil-war hatred – both sides could agree on the sacredness of the Rising. Indeed that was why it was so important to harness the symbolism of 1916 to current political causes. The GPO conferred legitimacy. Although the building figured in party-political wrangles, as an emblem of true Irish nationalism it was also a focus of attempts to establish political consensus throughout the middle years of the century. Impressed by the natural theatricality of the events of Easter week, in 1932 the playwright Denis Johnston suggested the inauguration of bank holiday re-enactments in Dublin, arguing that O'Connell Street was the perfect space for open-air drama: 'This street at the same time is the actual scene of certain events in our National history which provide a heroic theme as rich in dramatic values as anybody could wish. It is a theme which is outside the realm of controversial politics and which in fifty years' time will probably have become legendary.'

Drawing comparisons with traditional open-air performances such as *Jedermann* on the Cathedral Steps at Salzburg, or the *Attack on the Winter Palace* in Leningrad, Johnston proposed taking over 'the Street' from the Rotunda to the river in order to re-enact 'in conventionalised form the events of Easter Week 1916':

> It is suggested that the play should include the Fairyhouse crowds – the little band of marching men – the seizure of the Post Office – the Proclamation read at the foot of the Pillar – the charge of the Lancers – the closing in – the siege – the surrender – the Volunteers march out to prison and to death – fifteen men march ahead – the people follow.

Consider for a moment the value of such a play if it could be done successfully. It would be something unique in the world, apart from its personal value to the spectators.

Of course it would have to be done in the simplest way – quite short and to the point, with a little more elaboration when in the course of time it appeared what could be done and what could not. Years of patient experiment with constant cutting and alteration would be needed to perfect it as a spectacle. Perhaps the most serious problems would be to make it weather-proof. But none of these difficulties is insurmountable.

By 1932 Johnston was well known as a dramatist steeped in European modernist theatre, particularly the work of Strindberg. His phantasmagoric play *The Old Lady Says No!* had been produced in 1929 by Hilton Edwards at the Gate Theatre, having been rejected by the Abbey. An actor playing the national hero Robert Emmet is transported to the streets of modern Dublin, where he meets jobbing politicians, blind beggars, West Britons, prostitutes and a host of other characters in a series of scenes reminiscent of Joyce's 'Nighttown' sequence in *Ulysses*. The play clearly signalled its debts to O'Casey, as nationalist pieties were targeted head on, with contemporary politicians, now engaged in censorship and money-making, romancing about their days as gunmen:

MINISTER: And do you remember the day, Seamus, of the big round-up in Moore Street when the 'G' man tried to plug me getting out of the skylight? ...

O'COONEY: Aw, Jesus, and the evenings down in the old

I.R.B. in Talbot Street, picking out the 'Soldiers' Song' on the blackboard …

And that night waiting up on the North Circular for word of the executions. Ah, not for all the wealth of the world would I give up the maddening minglin' memories of the past …

Johnston published his plan for an open-air 'National Morality Play' in the Gate Theatre's journal *Motley* – a title that referred somewhat ironically to Yeats's poem 'Easter 1916' ('where motley is worn'). It is hard to believe that he meant this orgy of national sentiment seriously, but nearly ten years later – on the twenty-fifth anniversary of the Rising – he repeated his call for a street staging of the revolution in the liberal intellectual journal *The Bell*.

And however slyly tongue in cheek Johnston's proposal, it was debated seriously in the months that followed. There were several letters to the editor commending the proposal. A journalist for *The Leader* thought it a great idea but put forward the fear of influenza and 'the inability of the Irish public to take anything seriously' as possible drawbacks. Mary Manning, editor of *Motley* and a close friend of Johnston and Samuel Beckett, disagreed:

Did N. see the procession that marched to Glasnevin on Easter Sunday? Did she see the crowds that lined the streets to watch the Volunteers march past? There was no pageantry, no uniforms, no pomp, nothing to appeal to our sensations; nothing but the spirit of the thing, call it fanatical, call it anything you like – but one must pay allegiance to unbreakable devotion to an ideal. It seems to me that a section of the Public takes its Easter

Commemoration very seriously indeed, and that it would enter into the spirit of a National Morality play with all the necessary enthusiasm.

A section of the public were gung-ho for the Rising, yes, and those marching to the Republican plot in Glasnevin probably most of all. But an increasing problem even by the early 1930s was not disillusion with the outcome of the Rising, or party-political wrangling over ownership of 1916, but failure to remember it at all. At Easter 1932 the Gate put on a double bill of Pearse's *The Singer* and *Easter Week 1916* by Micheal MacLiammoir, described in the programme as 'Easter commemorative performances with a farcical interlude played with exhilarating verve'. One reviewer acknowledged that 'The crowded house listened to Pearse and MacLiammoir with the closest attention.' But he expressed the hope that 'When Easter 1916 is produced next year one would like to see an audience in vocal collaboration. But this is perhaps too much to expect from an Irish public which has forgotten "Let Erin Remember" and has never learned the National Anthem.'

As with the Rising itself, the problem was participation – the audience were quite willing to watch, but they wouldn't, or couldn't, join in. Normally unwelcome behaviour in the serious theatre-goer, the expectation of audience involvement was more usually associated with pantomime or music hall. But plays about the Rising were different. There was a feeling that 1916 theatre should be national in size as well as in theme. This was the point of Johnston's Morality Play, intended as a kind of politicised medieval pageant, with the Christian element already handily incorporated. Staging the Rising in front of the GPO would break down the boundary between stage and street, and render the audience actors in the drama, as they had so conspicuously failed to be fifteen years earlier. But this desire for the audience to finally join in – for the Rising to draw in more than the close circle of insurgents or politicians already intimately bound up in the events – spilled into the theatres themselves. Many of the 1916 plays of this period were conceived as street pageants squeezed on to an indoor stage. Michael MacLiammoir, for example, staged his 'Pageant of Dublin' every Easter, at the Mansion House, or at the Gate: 'The history of Dublin is vividly dramatised, from the invasion of the Vikings to Easter, 1916.' In later years these were recast as vast, televised spectacles in the Phoenix Park or the Royal Dublin Society grounds in Ballsbridge.

In seeking to narrow the distance between stage and street, dramatists were hoping for a re-enactment of the Rising that could fall just short of death and destruction (though the more ambitious reconstructions did involve building and then burning fake GPO facades). But as with the actual event, the audience had a tendency to be recalcitrant – they forgot their lines, or refused the parts assigned to them. In this sense the riots that greeted O'Casey's play in 1926 were to be commended. They proved at least that the audience were engaged, though it was true that the seats were taken by people who had played a part in the real thing: Margaret Pearse, Hanna Sheehy Skeffington. When Dublin theatre-goers couldn't recall the words to 'The Soldiers' Song' there was little danger of riots, but also of national enthusiasm and commitment.

It was difficult to get the right balance between spectating and participating in these staged reconstructions. It was a different matter with military parades, which offered a kind of ready-made communal theatre, bringing the actual participants in the Rising back on site to the GPO. From the relatively modest Easter Commemorations of the early years of the Free State a tradition of larger and larger public displays grew up; this was particularly the case after the victory of Fianna Fáil in the 1932 election, when Eamon de Valera took power. Easter Sundays during the 1930s saw the transformation of O'Connell Street into a national parade ground. Each year there were bigger and better viewing stands, fancier drapes. In this para-theatre of the Rising the massive height of the GPO and its grand columns were crucial. It was in this period that the outside of the building really gained its iconic status. After all, unlike, say, the storming of the Bastille, the major events at the GPO had taken place inside the building. But for the Rising to fulfil the demands of a national political display the street itself, and the ordinary Irish public, had to become part of the performance.

By far the largest number of photographs of the reconstructed GPO focus on these military parades. The march past the viewing platform, the massed ranks, the salute – the parades showcased military strength in a manner more associated with the twentieth century's totalitarian regimes than a small and ill-defended country. But the military display was intimately associated with the national meaning of the building, where Ireland's first soldiers had taken arms. Unlike the celebrations of the 4 July or 14 July, there was far less emphasis in Ireland on feasting and fireworks. The yearly commemorations were construed as a rededication of the state to the values of 1916 (the reading of the Proclamation; the solemn Mass), a quasi re-enactment. As the years passed, however, the need to draw a distinction between the politicians (the figureheads of the state), and the people, became increasingly important. Up until the early 1930s there was no viewing platform in front of the GPO – everyone who

marched did so as a participant in the events. With the introduction of the podium, the purpose of the marching army
was to show allegiance to the state.

All this only increased the political rivalry over ownership of the building. Alongside the steadily growing mountain of GPO recollections and souvenirs, politicians on both
sides of the civil-war divide battled to claim the legacy of
Easter week. Wrangles over invitations to military parades
in front of the GPO, and arguments over ever bigger and
better GPO publicity stunts, spilled out from the Dáil into
newspapers and journals. Given the emphasis on participation, the most pressing difficulty for the organisers of the
GPO parades was working out who should be invited. There
was nothing neutral about this. Soon after Fianna Fáil came
to power, for example, they excised 241 names from the
Cumann na Gaedheal list of invitees to the Easter week commemorations. When an outraged Richard Mulcahy asked
why men who had served in 1916 were no longer allowed to
join in the commemoration, Frank Aiken, the new Minister
for Defence, frankly admitted that the new government was
enjoying its power: 'People who fought in 1916 were delib-
erately excluded in the past. We have the compilation of this
list now and anyone who wants to get on the list will have
to satisfy us as to his claim.' A year later, with no agreement,
there were two sets of advertisements in the papers for rival
GPO marches. The Easter events were less commemorations
of the sacrifice of 1916 than party political demonstrations.

In 1932 Ireland applied to host the Olympic Games. To
those who suggested there was no venue large enough in the
capital to hold the expected numbers, wags pointed to the
GPO, which was surely Tardis-like in its ability to contain
the thousands who claimed to have served there. It was in

the run up to the twentieth anniversary that Diarmuid Lynch constructed his questionnaire, sending it out to several hundred people with whom he engaged in long correspondences – drawing maps, plans of the roof, even arranging meetings at Moore Street so that he could establish exactly what had happened during the evacuation. There were those who admitted quite frankly that they had come in to the GPO on the Monday but went home again; others clearly made up stories of their heroic activities that week. They had a financial incentive – inclusion in the 1916 Roll of Honour meant not simply medals and invitations to the commemoration parades, but state military pensions.

Tension gathered as the twentieth anniversary approached. It was obvious it was going to be a big thing, with all the opportunity for back-stabbing and in-fighting that this would afford. A slew of 1916-related publications were queuing up at the presses: memoirs, poetry, biographies, reprints of last speeches, photographic records and so on. National radio was planning a month of special programmes; all the papers and journals would bring out special editions. The most popular of these resembled reliquaries, catering to the almost inexhaustible appetite for 'authentic' records of the Rising, and best of all anything with a signature. The 1936 issue of the *Capuchin Annual*, for example, read like a reprint of the post-Rising issues of the *Catholic Bulletin*. There were eyewitness recollections, photographs of rebels and copies of documents: 'the last dispatch from the GPO', Pearse's farewell letter to his mother, the surrender note, the note from General Lowe. This gathering of artefacts was overlaid with mythic meanings as Frank Gallagher (editor of the *Irish Press*) extolled 'the movement which came out of the ruins of the GPO':

There was such pride in their pale and half-bearded faces, such dignity in the way they held themselves, that the ruins of Dublin's great thoroughfare and the acrid smell of burning wood made it seem like a place of ancient sacrifice from which those who were thought to be dead came forth with the seal of a divine mission on their foreheads.

And so it was: a nation that was dead had stirred upon its bier, had risen to disquiet timid men.

Given this sort of hype the opposition were determined make a stand on the GPO anniversary event, but so too were militant republicans who now held that de Valera too had betrayed the Republic by taking office in the illegitimate political entity that was the Free State. With the IRA now a proscribed organisation, there was a serious likelihood of trouble. De Valera's strategy for dealing with this was a bold one: he brought the lavish celebrations forward a year, so that the first really major GPO commemoration, which included the unveiling of a memorial inside the building, took place in 1935. It wrong-footed everyone.

Cumman na Gaedheal politicians reacted with fury in the Dáil at the use of the army for what was considered a party political demonstration; Maud Gonne MacBride hoped republicans would not go near the GPO on Easter Sunday (in fact they turned up there a little later to hold a counter-demonstration). But what the 'Easter Week Memorial Committee' pulled off was a festival of authenticity. As the *Irish Times* correspondent described the march past:

On they came, marching in military columns of four, some of them wearing the uniforms of the period of the

Rising which for years had been hidden against raiding parties of British soldiers. Others had a bandolier or a knap-sack – anything that was 'a relic of 1916' – and on their shoulders the men who were to fire the salute bore the old Mauser rifles, landed during the Howth gun-running by the late Erskine Childers.

De Valera's coup enabled him to avoid prolonged spats with the opposition over the commemoration, but also to take control of the meaning of the Rising. Arguably the only head of state able to reconcile the idea of the nation's revolutionary destiny with stable government (though not in the eyes of the IRA), he used the shows of military strength to signal not blood sacrifice but the battle for sovereignty. De Valera's version of modernity was less about savings banks than about the island's political future. In the first of his State of the Nation addresses against the backdrop of the GPO, de Valera made sure that the spirit of 1916 did the work of contemporary politics, arguing that 'only an Ireland free from foreign domination – North, South, East and West – would satisfy the aspirations of the Irish people'. Arguably he didn't have to worry so much about commerce and prosperity as much of that work had been done for him. Modern Dublin was very comfortable in its new commercial skin: cinemas, restaurants, crowds of shoppers, neon signs. In that context de Valera could safely return to the ideals first proclaimed at the GPO:

> This was the scene of an event which will ever be counted an epoch in our history – the beginning of one of Ireland's most glorious and sustained efforts for independence. It has been a reproach to us that the spot has remained so long unmarked. Today we remove that reproach. All

who enter this hall henceforth will be reminded of the deed enacted here. A beautiful piece of sculpture, the creation of Irish genius, symbolising the dauntless courage and abiding constancy of our people, will commemorate it, modestly indeed, but fittingly.

The memorial itself was certainly modest. A bronze cast of Oliver Sheppard's figure *The Death of Cuchulainn*, set on a plinth displaying a portion of the Proclamation, it was in no danger of overshadowing military theatricals in the street. The statue shows the mythological Irish hero, who single-handedly defended Ulster against an army from Connacht in the West, at the moment of his death on the battlefield. The perfect blend of the heroic and the *pietá*, the sculpture had been designed before the Rising, and it is quite possible that Pearse (whose father was a sculptor) had seen it.

The great thing about the Cuchulainn legend was that it could carry multiple meanings: 'a true type of Gaelic nationality, full as it is of youthful life and vigour and hope' according to Patrick Pearse; a symbol of service to the people before the self; a link to an ancient and noble Irish society. There were a few who wondered about the Ulster aspect of his lineage. As the *Irish Times* pointed out, it was 'somewhat paradoxical that the warrior who held so long the gap of Ulster against the Southern hordes should now be adopted as the symbol by those whose object it is to bend his native province to their will'.

The statue of Cuchulainn had obvious advantages over one of the individual heroic leaders. It didn't take much to imagine the battle between, say, Mrs Clarke and Mrs Pearse over which of their husbands should be immortalised in the GPO. It was not until the fiftieth anniversary in 1966 that

18. Detail of Oliver Sheppard's The Death of Cuchulainn. *Created in 1911–12, a bronze cast of the statue was unveiled in the Post Office in 1935. The symbolism of the image brings together the dead Christ of the Pietá with the ideal of heroic sacrifice extolled by Pearse.*

statues of the leaders were erected in Leinster House, the seat of the Irish Parliament. But the anonymity of the youth was important for other reasons: it signified the links between the generations. In a 1934 play, *The Conspirators*, Paul Vincent Carroll had imagined a group of nationalist statues (Parnell, Tone, Emmet, Mitchell and Fitzgerald) hearing the news of the Rising. They are able to gossip but not to move around, so that they are hopelessly out of touch with the new spirit in the country. By the end of play they have been joined by the dead son of the charwoman who has been gunned down in Stephen's Green. Carroll places an ordinary boy on a pedestal beside the heroes, rather than Pearse or Connolly, in a reprise in dramatic form of the Rising *pietá*. The image of a dying soldier with youthful Mother Ireland and angelic halo had been very popular after the Rising. *His Easter Offering* showed the young generation apotheosised in a glorious death. The Cuchulainn statue replayed similar elements in secular style, with the added benefit of forging a link between a mythic and a historical past – those who had died had taken their place in the ancient cycle.

Beyond that, of course, was the fact that Cuchulainn had managed to outlast his own death. As legend has it, mortally wounded he tied himself to a tree so that he could continue his fight; it was not until a raven perched on his shoulder that his enemies knew he was dead. The Cuchulainn of the statue is both dead and alive, the archetypical ghost or spirit of the Rising that lives on through the generations. As Yeats wrote in a late poem, 'The Statues':

When Pearse summoned Cuchulain to his side
What stalked through the Post Office? What intellect,
What calculation, number, measurement, replied?

Not everyone bought this line. In Beckett's 1938 novel *Murphy*, one of the characters, fresh from his latest amatory disaster, is observed in the hallowed hall of the Post Office:

… contemplating from behind the statue of Cuchulainn. Neary had bared his head, as though the holy ground meant something to him. Suddenly he flung aside his hat, sprang forward, seized the dying hero by the thighs and began to dash his head against his buttocks, such as they are.

Following an encounter with a Civic Guard of limited verbal means, Neary explains that he was overcome by 'the Red Branch bum' (though the Cuchulainn statue in fact has no bum: 'There is no rump ... How could there be? What chance would a rump have in the GPO?'). This was very different satire from O'Casey's, and indeed from Johnston's. It is easy to imagine how Beckett might have become exasperated with the mindless reverence with which the Rising was discussed in official channels and in twentieth-anniversary publications. His target in *Murphy* is not the corruption of the political class but the authority of the state as a whole.

The idea that Cuchullain was far more than a legendary figure was strangely confirmed thirty years later, during the preparations for the 1966 commemorations. The story goes that a woman from Granada Television called the Post Office and asked to speak to 'Mr Cotchlan'. When it was established that he was in fact a statue, she asked whether there was anything else in the Post Office connected with the Rising. Only two paragraphs from the Proclamation and the signatories, it was explained. The signatories? Could she speak to them?

⧖

From the mid 1930s onwards, GPO commemorations took on an increasingly military character, as de Valera worked hard to draw the connection between the state's founding moment and its developing independence from Britain. Soon after he came to power in 1932 he abolished the Oath of Allegiance to the Crown, and in a series of moves limited the power of the Governor-General. During the 1936 constitutional crisis, and the abdication of Edward VIII, the

Constitution Amendment Bill removed all reference to the monarch from the Free State Constitution. In the 1937 Constitution the name Irish Free State was dropped in favour of Eire, or Ireland (a term which formally designated all thirty-two counties). The country became a republic in all but name. The other side of this determined effort to consolidate and centralise power was crushing the IRA. The Fianna Fáil government introduced a number of repressive measures, including internment during the war. Under de Valera the GPO became a symbol of sovereignty – he paid lip service to the unfinished business of partition, while implying that independence had been achieved.

Certainly Fianna Fáil were not averse to making use of sentimental rhetoric about the Rising – particularly when directed at Irish Americans. The Irish pavilion at the New York World's Fair in 1939 sported an enormous carved granite pillar carrying a bust of the rebel leader Patrick Pearse in the centre. The pillar's design was ingenious: integrated within the granite were stone blocks taken from buildings that had almost sacred significance in the story of Ireland's struggle for independence. The pillar contained, for example, bits of the General Post Office; of Kilmainham Prison, where the rebels were held; and of Arbour Hill, where they lay buried. The whole construction was illuminated by the text of the 1916 Proclamation, in Irish and English.

But the GPO signified not so much sacrifice as strength. The first real change in the symbolism of the GPO occurred during the war, when the building began to signify a self-confident independent foreign policy, 'armed neutrality'. The frequent military displays performed in front of the GPO throughout the war years – and integrating the army, the Old IRA and the emergency services – were a form of communal theatre, emphasising the link between the rebellion of 1916 and the country's present fight for neutrality. In 1941, on the twenty-fifth anniversary of the Rising, de Valera cancelled the planned pageants and celebrations as inappropriate to the world situation but kept the march past, and made it grander than ever before. Twenty-five thousand men, many of them new recruits to the Local Defence Forces, marched past the GPO, along with all the tanks the army could muster: 'an entire nation prepared'. The year 1916 was figured as the precursor of Ireland's new self-assertiveness. The veterans were present as usual, but the emphasis was not so much on those who had fought as those now preparing to fight for their country. They were ready to take arms against either Britain or Germany, for this was billed as a 'war with both sides'.

The GPO thus symbolised determination to defeat Ireland's external enemies. But it also stood for the government's resolve to defeat its internal enemies – the IRA. In closely linking the GPO with the armed forces of the state, de Valera was claiming sole legitimacy for that army, in opposition to the claims of the IRA to be the legitimate heirs of 1916 and the true army of the nation. One of the paradoxes of the wartime emphasis on military strength was that it was designed to delegitimise the private army tradition, and thus demilitarise the political culture.

This re-orientation of the GPO towards sovereignty and away from sacrifice enjoyed a remarkable degree of success. Despite wartime paper shortages, the usual maudlin Rising memorabilia rolled off the presses for the twenty-fifth anniversary. The *Capuchin Annual*, for example, sported a very large section of recollections and photos of the Easter 1941 commemorations. These were set alongside the now

19. *A Pathé newsreel still, titled* Spectacular Parade in Dublin, *of the twenty-fifth anniversary commemorations at the GPO in 1941. The military display, including aeroplanes, mechanised troops, the nursing service, fire-fighters and civil defence services, passes the GPO, where de Valera takes the salute.*

familiar 1916 memorabilia: memoranda written in the GPO, last words, and so on. Much of this might have been published at any time over the last twenty-five years, and most of it had been. Indeed by this point it was hard to find new photographs, and the preference for printing Rising recollections by those who had become well-known statesmen, rather than the rank and file, meant that the store of new material was running very low. The radio station was criticised for churning out exactly the same stuff every year. But there were new elements to the twenty-fifth anniversary.

The first was the focus on an independent stance on the war. Neutrality during the First World War, and opposition to subscription, had been a central plank of Volunteer ideology, making it easy to draw comparisons with keeping out of the last war and keeping out of this one. The emphasis was on the Rising as a pacifist or at least anti-war event, despite the fact that it had depended on military action. There were frequent comparisons between the misleading propaganda about German atrocities then and now, suggesting that Ireland faced the same situation again, the need to confirm her independence through decisive action.

Donagh MacDonagh was two years old in 1916 when his father Thomas was executed as one of the leaders of the Rising. As a baby he featured in photographs published in the *Catholic Bulletin* focusing on the relatives left behind. For the twenty-fifth anniversary he produced a version of the by-now-typical Easter pageant for radio: 'Easter Christening, A Radio Masque'. It is Easter 1941 and a 'Seeker' wanders through Dublin looking for someone to speak to her of the spirit of revolution. She begins at the GPO:

> Perhaps where those ashes lie a spirit lingers.
> Beauty and sacrifice must leave a mark
> Upon the mould of nature. But at this building
> The very birthplace of their memory
> I can see nothing but the casual crowd.

In another reprise of the theme of revolutionary amnesia, the citizens of Dublin have reverted to Yeats's motley crowd, bent on getting and spending. Eventually, however, the Seeker comes across a few lone citizens who retain the spirit of 1916, including a mother who believes that it is better for her son to die than to leave, a soldier who says that the rebels speak under the clay, and a son who argues (handily) that the legacy of the Rising is Ireland's current sovereignty. MacDonagh recycled the well-worn images of transformation and generation:

Spring sowed in their bodies the seeds of rebellion;
We winnowed that crop, and the mind of all Ireland
Was changed in a season.

But the Rising was also credited with more tangible bequests, among them 'The sky free from menace'. There was sense in the argument that the Rising had helped keep Ireland out of not only one war but two, and in particular saved it from aerial bombing. Nonetheless, the repeated emphasis on the neutral state's martial prowess might be read – in the context of the world war – as protesting too much.

A comparison with the effect of the Second World War on European modes of commemoration may be instructive here. As historians such as Jay Winter have argued, the Second World War helped to put an end to the rich set of traditional languages of commemoration and mourning that flourished after the Great War. The year 1945 marked a deep caesura in European cultural life, as post-war art and 'rubble' literature recorded not the processes of healing, but the shock of violence done not only to numberless human beings, but to the very notion of humanity. Faith in progress, confidence in human decency, the sanctity of moral boundaries unbreakable even in war: all seemed to have suffered irreparable damage.

On the face of it a completely different dynamic was at

work in Ireland. Remembrance of the Rising had never been based on mourning and consolation – this had as much to do with the vast difference in numbers of dead as the determination to present 1916 as a willed and glorious action by specific heroic leaders. Moreover, in some sections of Irish society there was a tendency (compounded by strict wartime censorship) to interpret the Second World War as a rerun of the First, leading to a belief that Irish neutrality, symbolised by the country's new defensive rather than aggressive military strength, was 'superior' to the imperialist warmongering on the Continent. If anything, the war brought greater confidence to the claims made for the Rising, with the emphasis on heroic defence of the nation against imperial aggressors. With the majority of active IRA members interned and both sides in the civil war now standing side by side on the GPO podium, the events of 1916 and their aftermath were a point of consensus in the face of external threats. And oddly enough this new martial, rather than sacrificial, spirit was evident in some of the literary representations of the Rising that followed the war.

Liam O'Flaherty's novel *Insurrection* was a hymn to the heroism of pitched battle rather than sacrifice. Denis Johnston never did pull off his GPO street extravaganza, but in 1957 he wrote a play about the Rising which directly challenged O'Casey's pacifist protest in *The Plough and the Stars*. *The Scythe and the Sunset* is set in a café overlooking the Post Office on O'Connell Street. Unlike the majority of Rising representations there is no attempt at verisimilitude, nor at romanticism. As the Rising continues in desultory fashion in the GPO across the way, an imprisoned British officer and a nurse rig and fire a machine gun from the café, thereby wrecking the chance of negotiation and making sure the

Rising continues to the end. Neither of these characters is heroic, but they are fighters, and it is this trait that Johnston admires in them. In his version of the Rising it is not the executions that transform the situation but combat itself.

In his introduction to the play, Johnston gave a clue to another context which may have helped shape the new martial version of the events in the GPO: the post-imperial one. Although Ireland lost out internationally in the immediate aftermath of the Second World War, by the late 1950s the state had a strong presence at the United Nations. At the same time the post-war implosion of empire allowed a positive re-assessment of 1916. Listing Cairo, Delhi, Jerusalem and Nicosia, Johnston gave the prize for the first and best Rising to Dublin:

> The more one sees of how these uprisings have since been conducted elsewhere, the more reason everybody has to be pleased with Easter Week ... The passing of an imperial civilisation in which many of us were brought up is a process that has usually presented the same pattern – though not always so coherently – ever since the opening phase in Dublin. It is not an Irish but a world phenomenon, that the man who loses is often the man who wins, and that each side usually expends as much energy in playing the other fellow's game as it spends in furthering its own.

5

WHAT STALKED THROUGH
THE POST OFFICE?

*I do not think that there is anywhere in the country any bit-
terness about the events of 1916. I think that everyone, no
matter what shade of politics he belongs to, no matter what
party he supports, can join in appreciation of the sacrifices
and heroism of those men.*

Sean MacEntee, 1934

*Did you hear about this boy Pearse? The boy who took over
a post office because he was short of a few stamps ... He
walked in to post a letter and got carried away and thought
it was Christmas.*

Frank McGuinness, *Observe the Sons of Ulster Marching
Towards the Somme* (1986)

On Sunday, 10 April 1966 Frank Aiken, Minister for External
Affairs, arrived at Collins Barracks in Cork for the fiftieth-
anniversary commemorations of the Rising. The organisers
were keen to make good use of the largest military barracks
parade ground in Europe, and to that end had invited veterans to watch the march past of the Southern-based corps.
In order to have something suitably imposing for officers
and men to march past they had gone to some lengths to

20. An RTÉ newsreel still of the fiftieth anniversary commemoration in Collins Barracks, Cork, featuring a march past a mock-up of the GPO façade.

fit up a mock GPO, complete with pillars, windows, doors and viewing platform. The television footage of the event – watchable online – shows this contrived ceremonial collapsing into bathos. A tiny group of onlookers gather as an even tinier group of soldiers march past the diminutive GPO – looking like nothing so much as a cardboard stage set in an under-resourced amateur dramatic production – where a lonely-looking Aiken takes the salute. Later a soldier stands before the set to read the Proclamation. Everything that was to make the Dublin commemorations impressive, even moving, was absent from this event: crowds of onlookers, noise, massed ranks of soldiers and arms, and most of all the authentic granite facade of the GPO.

In the capital the veterans who joined the parade seemed to forge a tangible link between past and present. They were once again in the arena where the uprising occurred, in a shared public space that allowed the assembled citizens to feel they were participating alongside those who had helped to make those now-distant events. The contrast with the ritual in Ireland's second city could not have been greater. In addition to carrying the uncomfortable message that nothing worth remembering had happened in Cork in 1916, the parade was the ultimate in kitsch commemoration. The tacit referent of the event was not the Rising of 1916, but the ceremony taking place simultaneously in Dublin. It was a mock-up of a parade, as though the Dublin march past were the event to be celebrated – not the Rising itself. The fake GPO portico, intended as an inspiring emblem of the nation, conveyed an almost comic impression of flimsiness. One could just as easily imagine a parade past a replica of the burnt-out GPO – which might well have been more helpful to the historical imagination.

The idea of commemoration had taken on a self-referential life of its own. In provincial ceremonies up and down the country, children and young men stood on wooden platforms and in front of statues to read the Proclamation. As Cork's postmodern pastiche of a parade made clear, it was the ritual of commemoration, rather than the Rising itself, which was intended to bring the nation together.

Dublin had the advantage of the genuine portico, but it also made the most of authenticity in the shape of the veterans. The ranks of old soldiers were a tradition going back to the mid 1930s. But with the advent of television the commemorations made a fetish of them. The televised coverage of the ceremony in front of the GPO focused almost obsessively on

21. A Pathé newsreel still from 1938, Survivors of the 1916 Rising. *The newsreel featured the surviving members of the GPO garrison gathered together, with the GPO superimposed on them.*

the faces of survivors – their medal-wearing ranks swelled by men who had fought in the War of Independence. Overhead panning shots of the length of O'Connell Street and the height of the GPO were intercut with close-ups of their silent faces. The grey hair and lines of age were invested with an hieratic aura, as though these faces offered a tangible link with the past. In Louis Marcus's film about the Rising, *An Tine Bheo* ('The Living Flame'), which was brought out to accompany the commemorations, the camera slowly pans along the ranks of lined, unmoving, faces, and these shots were reproduced as photographs in the souvenir brochure 'Cuimhneacháin'. The rows of silent men stood as living witnesses to history, but also as a soldierly challenge to their descendants.

Alongside the faces of the old appeared the faces of the young. Schoolchildren, and pre-pubescent young men, were photographed reading the Proclamation from wooden platforms, or listening to it being read. Irish middle age was barely evident, except in the guise of a few politicians and high-ranking soldiers. And what was perhaps more striking, the only young adults who took part in the commemorations were members of the forces.

The presence of the children was hailed as proof of the 'continuity of history'. Radio interviews conducted at the children's parade at the end of the week focused on what Pearse's inheritance could mean to these young people. Several of the young interviewees were stumped for an answer, but the organisers of the week's events had done their best to provide them with one. Since the beginning of the year, essay competitions and school prizes had been encouraging the nation's young people to ponder issues such as which of the executed men was the best role model for the future, and what would 1916 mean in another fifty years. A series of radio and television plays for children (written by Bryan MacMahon) directly explored the relationship between the generations. The young lad in *A Boy at the Train*, for example, hears news of the Rising from a traveller down from Dublin. While the responsible adults all react with caution or disapproval, the boy runs to tell his ageing grandfather, the old Fenian, that the moment he has long waited for has come at last.

This play picked up on the trope of the moribund middle generation, which had been a mainstay of early representations of the Rising. The link is between the child and the old man, while everyone in between awaits resurrection by the inspiring deeds of the rebels. Yet this story of generational conflict and misunderstanding was for the most part turned on its head in the 1966 commemorations, which liked to stress continuity over rupture – the unbroken line of revolutionary history handed down from generation to generation.

The idea that Ireland's revolutionary energy was passed on in a kind of apostolic succession – 'Handing on the Torch' as one commemorative event proclaimed – came uncomfortably close to fulfilling a negative English stereotype of Irish history and politics. It was (and still is in some quarters) a common enough jibe that the Irish would happily swallow any tale of English cruelty and blindly follow the path of violence and destruction in the name of the 800-year history of persecution. In the opening scene of Frank Launder and Sidney Gilliat's 1946 film, *I See a Dark Stranger*, the young would-be revolutionary Bridie Quilty, played by Deborah Kerr, overhears her father telling tall stories of fighting in the GPO during the Rising. In reality he has never been to Dublin. The scene is set in a pub, with Bridie listening outside the bar-room. Drink is the leaven of her father's fantasies, which become in turn the source of his daughter's dangerous idealism: she hooks up with a German spy and intrigues for the overthrow of Britain. But all turns out well with Bridie, as she soon falls in love with a British officer and thus replaces her misguided and dangerous faith in her father with love for her steady and right-thinking husband. Part of the propaganda value of the film lay in the generational story, with its suggestion that mendacious hand-me-down histories were to blame for modern Ireland's inability to trust the British.

Those dangerous stories handed down through the

generations were more usually placed in the mouths of mothers, however. The 1966 BBC broadcast commemorating the Rising began with a litany of mothers who preached revolution to their sons. As Sean T. O'Kelly (who was in the GPO) explained, 'The songs meant everything. My mother used to sing patriotic songs ... My father wasn't very vocal. My mother was preaching to us children, she had seven children.'

These interviewees, men and women who had been active in 1916, might as easily have recalled their early consciousness of social and political injustice, if they had been asked about that. But they were asked about how their revolutionary consciousness had been passed on from the previous generation, and they were happy to answer accordingly because in fact the smooth generational story was vital to Irish constructions of 1916 in 1966. Not surprisingly this was a consequence of the fact that, at least as far as the guardians of the national consciousness perceived it, something had come unstuck between the generations; the torch was not being handed on after all.

Pageants, parades, masses, the renaming of streets and stations and unveiling of statues and most of all the television programmes on the Rising were all attempts to address the problem of the indifference of the young, by stressing the continuity of revolutionary patriotic endeavour. Participant accounts, long the staple of the yearly round of Easter commemorative publications, were given an extended lease of life as elderly men and women told their stories to screen. The emphasis was on immediacy, or 'making it live'. The RTÉ drama series *Insurrection* used the device of a 1916 television newsroom, complete with roving reporters who sent back interviews from inside the GPO. In drama as well as documentary the focus was on consultation with survivors, and indeed those who had not survived. The narrative frame for Bryan MacMahon's pageant for the Gaelic Athletic Association, *Seachtar Fear, Seacht Lá* ('Seven Men, Seven Days'), was that of a modern young Irish person addressing questions to the dead leaders, who helpfully used actors to answer for them.

The symbolism used to drive this message home was the phoenix flame. Because the Easter lily seemed tainted by its association with militant republicanism the government went for a new emblem: the sword of light. This combined with the symbolism of the GPO fire – everywhere apparent during 1966 – to suggest inspiration and rebirth but also continuity. This was the point of the 'living flame' of Louis Marcus's film, the phoenix rising from the flames in Oisín Kelly's sculpture (winner of the 1966 commemoration sculpture competition), the publications entitled 'Insurrection Fires at Eastertide'. What was being looked for was a reawakening of the spirit.

But for all the phoenix symbolism, the Taoiseach Seán Lemass was able to acknowledge that the kind of patriotic fervour looked for in 1966 was of a different order to fifty years before:

> The deeds that are required of Irishmen today are of a different kind dictated by a different phase of history. But the need for every Irishman and Irishwoman to accept his or her responsibility to the nation remains the same.

Eamon de Valera went further. Now President of the state, he was at the same time the most famous veteran of the Rising; indeed he seemed to quite enjoy his status

22. *The GPO does not appear in this image, but is implied in the conjunction of Pearse and phoenix flames. The image uses the famous portrait of Pearse from circa 1910. The profile hides the cast in his right eye, but the look also denotes farsightedness and firmness of purpose.*

23. A still from the RTÉ series Insurrection, *produced for the fiftieth anniversary of the Rising. Pearse says farewell to the burning building in the final moments in the GPO. The producers had clearly gone back to the illustrations in the 1916 issue of the* Irish Builder and Engineer *(illustrations 2 and 3) since the set includes the Telephone Silence Cabinet, though it does not feature in images based on the destroyed interior, such as Walter Paget's painting. Connolly's bed, looking surprisingly like a hospital issue, is also featured.*

as a kind of living relic of that transformative moment. In his speech at the closing ceremony he quoted President Kennedy's famous lines in which he had enjoined young Americans to ask not what your country can do for you, but what you can do for your country. The analogy was perfect, since it yoked together a young and resolutely modern generation, a once revolutionary past and a determinedly patriotic (and Cold War) stance. As Kennedy had put it, with scarcely veiled threats to the Russians: 'We dare not forget today that we are the heirs of that first revolution. Let the word go forth from this time and place, to friend and foe alike, that the torch has been passed to a new generation of Americans.'

The invocation of Kennedy was clearly intended to cast some of his iconic vigour over contemporary Irish youth, if not over the ageing de Valera himself. And like the youth of America, Irish young people were called on to join a battle that may have begun in revolutionary violence, but was now presented as securely economic. Despite the frequent complaints from clergy and an older generation of Irish politicians that the nation's young were hopelessly damaged by the individualism, financial greed and cosmopolitanism that were marks of modernity, most of the messages directed at them during the commemorations played on commerce. If, as Pearse had put it, 'every generation has its task', the task of the generation of 1966 as Lemass described it was 'to consolidate the economic foundations which support our political institutions, recognising that unless this is accomplished now the nation's future will always be in danger.'

The early 1960s had seen an element of economic growth in Ireland, a small fall in emigration and a rise in the number of marriages and children. To capitalise on this mini-boom, as many critics and historians have noted, social and economic transformation took over from the anti-partition campaign as the focus of national endeavour. Economics had long been a focus of patriotism, of course, but the Fianna Fáil mantra had for many years been protection. Now, with the European Economic Community in its sights, the government promoted competition and enterprise as the new basis for economic nationalism.

The anniversary also aimed at bringing in money from abroad. Tourism had been a major focus of 1916 commemorations right through the 1950s, when the spring festival An Tóstal', inaugurated in 1953, attempted to lengthen the short summer season by bolting on a range of Easter events. This was augmented in 1966 by the Easter Rebellion Anniversary Tour, designed for American tourists. Likewise the commemorative issue of the *Irish Digest* interspersed rousing tales of the spirit of 1916 with advertisements for travel and industry. The differences between George Morrison's 1959 film *Mise Éire*, and his remake for 1966, which was funded by the Department of Foreign Affairs, provided one index of the new mood. *The Irish Rising 1916* replayed the Eisenstein-influenced montages of newsreels from the 1916 period and Sean O Riada's symphonic versions of traditional airs. But the film concluded with a montage of modern commercial Dublin (Ringsend Generating Station, Finglas Transformer Station, RTÉ Studios). The general aim was to focus international eyes on contemporary Ireland – it was supplied to eighty networks and television stations worldwide, with a script that could be read by a local narrator – but the specific targets were US and European businesses.

Whatever Irish-American businessmen thought, the government seems to have been astoundingly unsuccessful in persuading its own citizens of its new go-ahead identity. Certainly the GPO parades themselves were impressive. The opening ceremony managed to combine dignity (the veterans) and popular enthusiasm (cheering crowds, brass bands) with political seriousness – lent as much by the cultured tones of actor Maurice O'Doherty's reading of the Proclamation as by the presence of de Valera himself. The volley fired from the roof of the GPO in the closing ceremony was undoubtedly stirring. There is ample anecdotal evidence that children did know a great deal more about the Rising after Easter week than before it, though for large numbers this probably did not amount to much more than swapping a rebel slouch hat for a cowboy one (or as Fintan O'Toole recalls, confusing the seven leaders with the Magnificent Seven). Citizens young and old were drawn into events, at least as long as they lasted. But they did not last long. Rather like the Pope's visit to Ireland in 1979 – heralded at the time as proof of a massive devotional tide washing through Irish society but understood in retrospect as the last gasp of the unquestioned authority of the Church – the 1966 national display was less a reaffirmation of patriotic values than a final wave goodbye.

Peter Lennon's 1968 film *The Rocky Road to Dublin* showed the soft underbelly of the commemorations. Banned after a short run, the film explicitly targeted the failure of the national project and the disillusion of ordinary citizens in Dublin. Both commentary and interviews – particularly those with the writer Sean O'Faolain and the critic and politician Conor Cruise O'Brien – stressed the population's disenchantment with the political and clerical elite. As Peter Lennon's commentary put it, Ireland faced 'the old problem of what to do with your revolution once you've got it.' The generation born in the 1930s had been brought up as the sons and daughters of revolutionary heroes. Rather than being encouraged to emulate their parents' generation the role allotted them was one of 'unquestioning gratitude' and 'heroic obedience'. 'Whatever had been poetic about our revolution had faded and there was no longer a trace of socialism … We lived in the shabby afterglow of heroic days that had long since faded.'

When Sean O'Faolain lamented to camera the loss of the

'spirit of 1916' he was echoing militant republican sentiment since 1922 – even to the extent of repeating the line that 'if those sixteen dead men of 1916' were to return today and see the kind of Ireland that had come out of their sacrifice they would feel it had all been in vain. What was striking was that this argument was hitched not to an appeal against partition, but to an explicit call for modernity, liberalisation and international social justice.

The popular mythology of Irish social change in the early twentieth century was of a battle between religion and materialism, between rural and urban existence, national culture and cosmopolitanism, tradition and modernity. These handy dichotomies were bandied about by those both for and against change. It is true that in 1960s Ireland, and particularly in Dublin, the tension between modernising 'external' influences (particularly popular music and television) and the mores of a traditional, and clerically controlled, society were acute. The younger generation were at the forefront of negotiating these tensions. A year after the jubilee, in 1967, the reform of the censorship laws, and of the education system pointed to the pressures that had been building within the system.

But the idea that the young (those who had not been forced to emigrate) were turning away from the patriotic message of 1916 because they were caught up in the materialist values of modern consumer society was too simplistic. The problem with the national story was not so much that it was too nationalist, but that it was empty of ideals. The economic ideas powering integration into the Common Market were new; but the party machine that presented them to the public was the same. Those who reacted with indifference, or even hostility, to the 1966 commemorations were – at least in part – registering their impatience with the ways in which the revolution was being manipulated for Fianna Fáil's political and economic programme. Ironically, given their reputation as the materialist generation, what they minded was that 1966 was all about money, that modern politics was determined above all by economic criteria. There was a brief scandal when a university student intervened on the popular RTÉ discussion programme *The Late Late Show* to declare that contemporary bourgeois Ireland had betrayed the ideals of the 1916 Proclamation. The national independence movement had become merely another political party: a bunch of 'celebrating hucksters' as the writer Máirtín Ó Cadhain dubbed them. The flurry of support for the Labour Party in 1968 reflected the impact of international civil rights and student movements in Ireland, as did the short-lived vogue among left-wing university students for joining the Official IRA. As the movement against the Vietnam war grew in the United States, so did the frustration of those in Ireland who saw the state's independent stance on foreign policy collapsing under clerical pressure to join the Cold War crusade. The government was worried about the indifference of the young, but it would have been more apt to call it political disillusion. The heroic idealism of 1916 had been sold.

In one of the longest sequences of Lennon's film the camera plays on the faces of young adults listening to a traditional music session in a pub. The scene unfolds in real time and with a kind of raw realism that gives the viewer the sense of being part of the cramped gathering. The sequence is about social change – there are women in the pubs, for a start, and they are enjoying themselves. But it is also about continuity: they listen to Irish music, not British or American imports. It was a form of continuity that lay in direct contrast to that of the 1916–66 story of revolutionary rebirth. The ranked faces of the veterans, 'grey heads and grey faces' as one student magazine described them, had no place there. At least one politician seemed to understand this. In November 1966 Lemass announced his resignation with an explicit acknowledgement that the generation gap had grown too wide:

> I believe ... that it is right that the representatives of the newer generation should now take over ... The 1916 celebrations marked the ending of a chapter in our history and a new chapter has now to begin. As one of the 1916 generation, this marked the end of the road for me also.

⌛

Celebrations of revolution by established governments carry their own ironies. The most successful are able to harness the idealism and creativity of the originary moment to enhance their own legitimacy: the underlying claim is that the contemporary political institutions and social life of the state embody the hopes of the revolutionary generation. Conversely, it's not hard to see the subversive potential of anniversaries, which can just as easily draw attention to the ways in which those revolutionary hopes have been betrayed. In 1966 that subversive potential played out very differently north and south of the Irish border.

Two years before appearing in Lennon's film, a youngish Conor Cruise O'Brien had argued for disillusion over indifference in the young. Rather than a fully-fledged regenerating fire, contemporary Irish men and women were living among 'the embers of Easter'. Like many, he took the opportunity of the anniversary to assess what had been achieved: a sovereign state, with soldiers in green honouring the dead leaders of 1916, but having abandoned the national, cultural and social objectives that had impelled them to fight against British imperialism. 'It even seemed possible at one stage that Ireland might have something distinct and useful to say in relation to revolution in the under-developed world, and the attitude of the advanced world towards revolution. These hopes were to fade.' O'Brien argued that the failure of the Republic had been inevitable – from its very beginnings the state's existence had constituted a violation of republican principles. The dictates of pragmatic politics had created an English-speaking state, where partition was accepted. 'But our dissatisfaction was deepened by the long-continued effort to keep alive the illusion that something was being done about the reunification of the country.' It was, O'Brien insisted, in the gap between official praise for the socialist and republican ideals of Pearse and Connolly, and the abandonment of those ideals by a conservative clerical establishment, that disillusion grew.

O'Brien's position was to change radically. Writing after the resurgence of violence in Northern Ireland, he condemned the 'cult of 1916' for fostering that violence. 'The great commemorative year' was

> ... a year in which ghosts were bound to walk, both North and South ... The general calls for rededication to the ideals of 1916 were bound to suggest to some young men and women not only that these ideals were in practice being abandoned – through the Lemass-O'Neill meetings and in other ways – but that the way to return to

them was through the method of 1916: violence, applied by a determined minority.

By the mid 1990s the socialist and anti-imperialist aspects of the Rising had disappeared from O'Brien's stance, and he condemned it outright as the fruit of Pearse's mystical nationalism based on blood sacrifice: 'But the Proclamation was not only the signal for an immediate once-off blood-sacrifice, claiming all its signatories and many others. It was also a blessing on an indefinite number of further blood-sacrifices, in order to attain a kind of sacral-political Second Coming: the ultimate terrestrial advent of the Republic proclaimed at Easter 1916.' Instead of embers, O'Brien's favourite metaphor for the afterlife of the Rising became ghosts. The dead of the rebellion were unquiet ghosts that must be appeased by recurrent sacrifices, an endless cycle in which the dead generations must be fed with the blood of the living. This gothic symbolism – a nation sacrificing its own, the tyranny of the dead – entirely displaced the symbolism of spirit and living flame in the decades that followed.

There was a core of O'Brien's argument about 1916 which remained constant, however – and this was the relationship between 'reality' and 'idealism'. The accusation was that both political parties had, over long years, encouraged sentimental fantasies of a united (and Irish-speaking) Ireland, even while they were engaged in the practical politics of integrating the state culturally and economically with Britain and Europe. After the start of the Troubles, the accusation became more pointed. The cult of heroic sacrifice was, even if indirectly, the cause of sectarian violence in the North.

It was true that, despite the drive to represent the nation as modern and forward-looking, the 1966 commemorations did not avoid republican mantras. De Valera's speech at the closing ceremony was the most famous statement of irredentism that year. His admission that 'I, for one, am never going to believe that the land of the O'Neills, the Ó Catháins, the McDonnells, the Maguires and McGuinesses, that that land is going to remain permanently severed from the rest of this country' was capped by a heart-stopping volley of rifles from the roof of the GPO, which could certainly be interpreted as armed defiance. But de Valera's speech was not the only example of what would later be called 'old-style nationalism'. The jubilee pageant 'Aiséirí' (Resurrection) was modelled on the 1916 pageants that Michael MacLiammoir had started at the Gate in the early 1930s and that had become a feature of yearly Easter celebrations during the An Tóstal festivities in the mid 1950s. (The pageants had shifted from the cramped Gate stage to the Phoenix Park, bypassing the O'Connell Street re-enactments dreamed of by Denis Johnston.) Like its predecessors, Aiséirí' presented scenes from revolutionary history from 1798 to the present. The final scene of the pageant addressed the citizens of the North as those who 'remain forever our own people' to the accompaniment of the tricolour and the music of 'A Nation Once Again', though the fact that this irredentist statement was made in Irish meant that many of the people watching would not have understood it. In pamphlets and publications directed towards Irish-American visitors, Seán Lemass repeated the goal of re-unification – it was the least that was expected.

But beyond these direct anti-partition statements lay the emotional impact of the story of the Rising as a whole. The TV series *Insurrection* was intended to be both well-crafted drama and a historically respectable account – RTÉ co-opted a leading academic historian as an adviser. The story that it told was not straightforwardly heroic – the Volunteers are represented as tired and often frightened men, local Dubliners are shown as uninterested in the Rising, there is a sympathetic portrait of Eoin MacNeill. Most of all, the blood-sacrifice elements were toned down in the series; the men in the GPO are waiting for reinforcements. Yet this determination to offer a balanced account did nothing to lessen the emotional impact of the series. As the novelist Colm Tóibín has recalled of his childhood experience of watching the series with his family, 'The executions were drawn out, each moment dramatised – the grieving family, the grim prison, the lone leader in his cell, writing his last poem or letter. Sometimes the emotion in our house was unbearable, and when it came to James Connolly's turn to be executed my mother ran out of the room crying.' Tóibín then makes the astonishing admission, for a ten-year-old, that it was the first time he had seen his mother cry.

It became fashionable during the worst years of the Northern crisis – particularly in the United Kingdom – to target republican myth-making as the cause of it all. In fact this critique of the Rising was embedded in Southern intellectual discourse long before the start of the Troubles. By the mid 1960s there was a growing movement within Irish historical studies concerned to interrogate the popular understanding of the Rising, and confront it with professional historical analysis. There was nothing discreet about this goal. The historian F. X. Martin argued of his edited collection *Leaders and Men of the 1916 Rising* that it attempted to transfer 1916 'from the realm of mythology to the realm of history'. What was needed was fewer plaques to the memory of the heroes, and more historical scholarship.

Martin presented the problem as a battle between history and myth. Listing the titles of popular 1966 publications about the Rising (*Deathless Glory*, *The Glorious Seven*, *Sixteen Roads to Golgotha*, *Our Own Red Blood*, *Cry Blood*, *Cry Erin*) he argued that:

> it has not been academic historians, nor even the James Stephenses and the Stephen McKennas but the Brian O'Higginses who have directly influenced the political views of Irish youth between 1917 and 1963. The Pearse-O'Higgins view of Irish history may be inaccurate (simply because it is one-sided) but it has sent young men out to die more certainly than did the Cathleen ni Houlihan of Yeats.

The young men he had in mind were men like Seán South and Fergal O'Hanlon, killed on New Year's Day 1957 in a raid on an RUC barracks in Brookeborough, County Fermanagh. The IRA's border campaign was called off in 1962, due to a lack of popular support, yet the young volunteers were romanticised in popular songs such as this one, which recalls Francis Ledwidge's elegy for Thomas MacDonagh ('He shall not hear the bittern cry/In the wild sky, where he is lain'), and which was later sung by the Wolfe Tones:

> No more he will hear the seagull's cry,
> Or the murmuring Shannon tide.
> For he fell beneath a northern sky
> Brave O'Hanlon by his side.
> They have gone to join that gallant band
> Of Plunkett, Pearse, and Tone.
> Another martyr for old Ireland,
> Sean South from Garryowen.

There was a sense in which arguing for the dangerous power of the myth of the rebellion was buying into the rebels' own hype: that idealistic belief in the nation might conquer the might of the British Empire. Most people in the GPO, however, had believed at some level that their actions made military sense, particularly in the context of the world war. In arguing that the idea of blood sacrifice had overwhelmed rational thought, the historians were not thinking historically. They were reflecting back on events the republican myths that grew up in response to them. This went along with an attempt to rehabilitate Eoin MacNeill. For decades MacNeill's countermanding order had been blamed for the failure of the Rising; new documents showed that MacNeill had been the victim of deception, and that the order was not given on a destructive whim, but an honest assessment of the chances of success. Though MacNeill had been no supporter of Home Rule, bringing him in from the cold was also part of recovering Home Rule as a viable political option. The Rising had been a bad idea: it had entrenched divisions with Northern Protestants; acted as a catalyst for the War of Independence; and caused partition, the civil war and now war in the North.

These views hardened as the situation in Northern Ireland worsened, particularly after Bloody Sunday, when sectarian murder and tit-for-tat killings were part of the daily news. Critics of the Rising, and of Rising commemorations, felt they were responding to the violence that had been unleashed, and to the continuing use of the language of 1916 by militant republicans, who claimed kinship with the revolutionary ideals espoused by Pearse. As Garrett FitzGerald had put it in 1966, 'the spurious claims made by propagandists for extreme nationalism ... have contributed to a growing cynicism about the national movement of 1916 and the years that followed.'

But the critics were also responding to the way in which discussions of the Rising had become polarised into arguments for dream or myth on one side and politics or rationality on the other. What was striking was the way the rebels' idealism had transmuted over the years. In the immediate aftermath of the Rising their idealism had been evident through their hopeless bravery against overwhelming odds, the 'nobility' and honour they brought to the fight. They had been misguided but they were honest. For the international left their idealism was evident in the socialist and anti-imperialist elements in the ideology of the Volunteers, and particularly in Connolly's writings. In the wake of the executions, and the religious discourse that greeted them, the rebels' idealism had been equated with a kind of mystic willingness to sacrifice themselves for the nation. This was the interpretation which stuck.

The debate about mythic blood sacrifice was also an opportunity for history to square up to literature. The literary elements of the Rising – the staged drama at the GPO, the impetus for rebellion found in the theatre of the cultural revival, the poetic manifestos produced by Pearse, Plunkett and MacDonagh – had always had a place in assessments of the event. Indeed, the intimate connection between literature and revolution had formed a central core of public celebrations of the Rising down the years. Pageants and spectacles like those by Donagh MacDonagh and Bryan MacMahon interwove poetry and political pronouncements into a (nearly) seamless whole. We might see this as an attempt to bring both the history and the literature of the nation together in one performance. But it was also a consequence of the fact that the literary take on the Rising – not only Pearse's lines in 'The Mother' but Yeats's equivocal 'Easter 1916' and O'Casey's play – were all quickly recognisable ways of 'tagging' meanings on to the Rising. Literature had become part of the event, and it was a quick way in for those given the task of representing it.

It was also a quick way of undermining the Rising. In 1967, for example, literary scholar William Irwin Thompson published a study of the literary aspects of the Rising entitled *The Imagination of an Insurrection*. Thompson's line was that the 'imagination' of revolution, the revolutionary idea, had overwhelmed rational political thought. Focusing on the revolutionary aesthetic in works by the writers associated with the Rising (Pearse, Plunkett and MacDonagh), he argued that the event had seen political action moulded by an exercise of artistic will (rather like Daniel Corkery's dramatised argument in his 1918 play *Resurrection*).

In fact the criticism of the Rising for its literary (and therefore irrational) roots was more subtle than outright condemnation of all writerly associations. To an extent critics of the Rising were engaged in a debate about literary value. To return to Pearse's joke that the Rising might get rid of a bunch of bad poets, it was the association with indifferent poetry that revealed the poverty of Rising politics. At the beginning of his 1959 film documentary *Mise Éire*, George Morrison had intercut photographs of Yeats and Pearse. This montage reproduced in visual form the standard line that Yeats's play *Cathleen ni Houlihan* had acted as a catalyst for revolutionary action (in Yeats's words, it had sent out certain men the English shot), and that this had set in train all subsequent Irish history. But for critics of the Rising in the 1960s and 1970s there was a clear need to disentangle critical literature (for example Yeats and O'Casey, but also literary novels such as Iris Murdoch's *The Red and the Green* or Walter Macken's *The Scorching Wind*) from literary myth (for example Pearse, but also the mass of popular fictions, heroic fighting narratives, amateur histories and sentimental histories of sacrifice). F. X. Martin put it quite explicitly: Pearse's own interpretation has persisted above that of O'Casey, Behan or O'Flaherty, and this was to be lamented. What has become known as the 'revisionist' turn in Irish history was deeply suspicious of popular culture.

It was difficult then to know how to read Seamus Heaney's Rising commemoration. His poem 'Requiem for the Croppies' was written on the fiftieth anniversary of the 1916 Rising, and it cannot be easily categorised either as the poetry of popular sentiment (though it has been voted most popular Irish poem on several occasions) or as critical of the myth of recurrent revolution.

> The pockets of our greatcoats full of barley –
> No kitchens on the run, no striking camp –
> We moved quick and sudden in our own country.
> The priest lay behind ditches with the tramp.
> A people, hardly marching – on the hike –
> We found new tactics happening each day:
> We'd cut through reins and rider with the pike
> And stampede cattle into infantry,
> Then retreat through hedges where cavalry must be
>   thrown.
> Until, on Vinegar Hill, the fatal conclave.
> Terraced thousands died, shaking scythes at cannon.
> The hillside blushed, soaked in our broken wave.
> They buried us without shroud or coffin.

And in August the barley grew up out of the grave.

On the surface an elegy for those killed in the Battle of Vinegar Hill in 1798, the poem brings together a version of the Kathleen ni Houlihan myth (bloodletting renewing the earth) with the iconography of the poppy – the seed which grows from the waste of battle. The image of the seed suggests that rebellions occur in a natural cycle of renewal (in January 1916, Connolly had written, 'We have planted the seed, in the hope and belief that ere many of us are much older, it will ripen and blossom into action.') The barley provides sustenance for later generations. Heaney later stopped including the poem in his readings, fearing it would be taken as an endorsement of IRA violence. But his explanation of the impulse behind the poem suggests the need for a far more subtle reading: 'I think the young nationalist in me was trying to give voice to things that the culture in Northern Ireland did not admit. There was no official space for anything of that kind.' The poem registers the official suppression of 'memories' and discussion of the Rising in the North, while in the South the young were protesting the official stitch-up of authorised versions of the Rising, which allowed little space for discussion either; official sanction and official veto mirrored each other.

⌛

Arguably the most important interpretation in 1966 of what had happened in the GPO was Ian Paisley's. Despite fears of public disorder if republican commemorations went ahead (1966 was also the fiftieth anniversary of the Somme), the Stormont government allowed a march through West Belfast, and other local events. The assent of Northern Ireland Prime Minister Terence O'Neill to these Northern commemorations worried Ulster loyalists because it appeared to be the next step in giving republicans a political voice. There was already considerable anger over O'Neill's ecumenism, and the cross-border talks with Taoiseach Seán Lemass. A key group had been involved in establishing a new Ulster Volunteer Force, in imitation of the original force founded in 1913. Paisley responded to the 1916 commemorations by holding a counter-rally at the Ulster Hall in Belfast, to celebrate 'the defeat of the rebels in 1916'. Tensions ran very high and a few days after the counter-rally the UVF declared war on the IRA.

Northern republican invocations of 1916 and the GPO had little to do with the official rhetoric of the Rising in the South. Proclamations about the future economic progress of the state had nothing to say to them, who were not part of that state. The 1916 marches and rallies that were held in the North were about confirming a sense of belonging to the Irish nation, and proclaiming a distinct Northern nationalist and local identity. In the broader context of political change in the mid 1960s, including the new Labour government in Britain, it was precisely this that spooked Ulster Unionists.

The return to the rhetoric of 1916 at the start of the Troubles should be understood against the backdrop of the growing violence in Northern Ireland throughout 1969, as conflict over the movement for civil rights led to increasingly violent clashes between Protestant and Catholic communities in Belfast and Derry, including riots and burning people out of their homes, and culminated in the deployment of British troops in the summer of 1969. In mid August 1969 a particularly brutal period of violence in Catholic Belfast left eight dead over two days, and Bombay Street 'burning from end to end'. This prompted those republicans dissatisfied with the leftward trend within the IRA (and the decision to drop parliamentary abstentionism) to walk out and form a new paramilitary organisation, the Provisional IRA.

Just as in 1922, during the crisis over the treaty, in 1969 the symbolism of 1916 again lay at the heart of internal battles within the republican movement. Like republican groups before them, the Provisionals drew their legitimacy from the actions which took place at the GPO. In their first public statement in December 1969 they announced: 'We declare our allegiance to the thirty-two county Irish republic, proclaimed at Easter 1916, established by the first Dáil Eireann in 1919, overthrown by force of arms in 1922 and suppressed to this day by the existing British-imposed six-county and twenty-six-county partitioned states.'

The Provisionals were affirming the military rather than parliamentary political role of the IRA – the aim was not to campaign for seats in parliamentary governments (either North or South), but to abolish them. The violence of August 1969 seemed to prove the uselessness of a political strategy, as it underlined the failure of the Stormont government to protect the citizens of Northern Ireland. The burning of Bombay Street gave rise to the symbolism of the phoenix flame – 'out of the ashes of Bombay Street arose the Provisional IRA', or as one mural in West Belfast has it, 'Out of the Ashes of "69" arose the Provos'. Certainly the burning of Catholic Belfast was the catalyst for the image of the phoenix, yet the living flames, burning GPOs, and risen phoenix that had formed such a central part of the 1966 commemorations of the Rising in the Republic were also present. The rebirth and resurgence of the ideals of 1916 was recast in explicitly military terms by Northern republicans (prompting critics such as Conor Cruise O'Brien to respond with the symbolism of blood sacrifice).

The image of the phoenix rising from the ashes dated from the 1970s, yet it was in 1981 that the rush of phoenix murals began to appear on the streets of Catholic areas of Belfast and Derry. Their purpose was to link the rebirth of militant republicanism (the Provisionals arising from the ashes of Bombay Street) with the powerful iconography of the hunger strikes, when ten men died in a protest against the criminalisation of republican prisoners by the British government.

Northern republicans have described the hunger strikes as 'the 1916 of our generation'. Part of the analogy rests on the way these strikes, like the Rising, revitalised the republican movement. As Martin McGuinness put it in 1987, 'Not since the declaration in arms of the Irish Republic on the steps of Dublin's GPO in 1916 has any event in modern Irish history stirred the minds and hearts of the Irish people to such an extent as the hunger strike of 1981.' Another member of contemporary Sinn Féin, Jim McVeigh, who is a former prisoner of the H blocks, expands:

Well I think it is true to say that they represented the 1916 of our generation. They radicalised both the older and younger generations. Tens of thousands of young people got involved at the time. What really puts this in perspective is a very famous picture of a group of young people gathered at Martin Hurson's graveside. Years later many of these people had been imprisoned or were dead. It was a monumental event and had a huge effect on public opinion. It brought a whole new generation into the struggle.

The invocation of 1916, the rhetoric of regeneration, the apparent approval of the 'feeding' of the dead generations with young people – this is the kind of rhetoric that has led critics to condemn the ideology of blood sacrifice at the heart of the republican movement, and to argue that the Rising itself has acted as a blight on rational political argument and the democratic structures of government. The opposition seems to be as stark as that described by Yeats in 'Sixteen Dead Men', between the language of 'give and take' and the ghostly logic of MacDonagh's bony thumb. It is certainly the case that the Rising was used as a legitimating narrative by the Provisionals, and the symbolism of quasi-religious martyrdom, of victory rising from defeat and of popular radicalisation all suggest ways in which the rhetoric of 1916 may have had deleterious effects.

Yet the analogy between the Rising and the hunger strikes was a reasonable one in some respects. Just as the Rising had not been intended as a bloody rout, so the hunger strikes too began as a 'rational' protest, or one that had a rational element. The prison protests had begun in 1976, when 'Special Category' status began to be phased out for newly convicted prisoners. Special Category effectively acknowledged the political nature of the prisoners' convictions, and the British government were unhappy with it as it reinforced the paramilitaries' idea of themselves as engaged in a legitimate struggle. In September 1976 the first prisoner to be convicted under the revised rules refused to wear prison uniform. He was not supplied with civilian clothing and was therefore confined to his cell in the H blocks at HMP Maze/Long Kesh. As more prisoners went 'on the blanket' the authorities responded with loss of privileges (no TV, radio, books or remission of sentences).

The protest escalated to the 'no wash' and then the 'dirty' protest, when prisoners refused to slop out their cells. A war was now taking place inside the prisons. In October 1980 the prisoners announced a hunger strike for political status, which was led by Brendan Hughes and six other men. (A previous hunger strike by prisoners in Crumlin Road Gaol in 1972 had succeeded in gaining the same status for those prisoners as the internees at Long Kesh, so there was a precedent for the strike as a practical and effective action.) This hunger strike was called off early in 1981, but concessions from the prison authorities were not forthcoming, and this perceived 'betrayal' by the authorities precipitated a second hunger strike, led by Bobby Sands. The British government under Margaret Thatcher refused to concede the prisoners' demands and the second strike was called off only after the deaths of ten men. Despite the iconography of the suffering Christ that was associated with the hunger strikes, and the rhetoric of sacrifice for the nation, the protest was not initially intended as a willing embrace of death. Arguably, too, the language of religious martyrdom in which the strikers' deaths were described should be understood not so much as a way of framing their actions as a way of responding to, and dealing with, their tragic deaths.

Throughout the hunger strikes the GPO was used as the focal point for republican protest in the South – protest directed against Britain but also against the Fianna Fáil government for failing to support the prisoners. Like Internment in 1971, and Bloody Sunday in 1972, the hunger strikes did garner a large amount of support for the republican movement south of the border (in each case republicans could be seen as victims rather than perpetrators of violence). Initially a focus for thousands of protestors, Sinn Féin used the GPO rallies to hand out leaflets and information about the strikes, in order to get round the media news blockade. In the election of June 1981 two prisoner candidates were elected to the Dáil, and the Fianna Fáil government fell. Yet as the protest continued, and it appeared that the British government was not going to climb down, Southern support for the strikers fell away and numbers at the GPO rallies dwindled.

Throughout this period, official government rhetoric in the South had stepped back from the Rising; the yearly Easter commemorations outside the GPO were discontinued in an atmosphere where any celebration of the Rising, particularly a military parade, could be construed as support for the continuance of armed struggle in the North. Arguably, however, this abandonment of the GPO by the government left the way clear for militant republican interpretations of the Rising, which stressed the legitimacy of the Provisionals as the heirs of the first Volunteers, and traced their mandate back to the declaration of independent sovereignty for the whole island, in the Proclamation of the Republic. In 1991 there was anger at the decision not to mark the seventy-fifth anniversary of the Rising, particularly from those on the left.

At the same time, as the Troubles dragged on through the 1980s, 1916 and the GPO became less and less important to Northern republicans. The political and symbolic memory of Northern republicans has become a 'six counties' memory – commemorations focus on the Maze rather than the GPO, the people remembered are those who have died in the North, rather than Pearse and Connolly. In 2002, for example, Sinn Féin announced an Easter Rising commemoration that was to take the form of a tribute to 'the families of IRA Volunteers, Sinn Féin activists and other republican activists' killed in recent times, 'a commemoration and celebration of those patriots'. The construction of a Northern imagination of the political struggle has meant that the GPO has been left behind except insofar as the legitimacy claimed for the armed struggle continues to stem from the Rising. Invocations of the GPO have more to do with saving face than with a genuine argument about political legacy and tradition.

In keeping with this shift, republican murals fuse images of the GPO with the contemporary struggle. A mural in Whiterock Road, Belfast, based on an image by artist Bobby Ballagh, shows the GPO and the seven signatories to the Proclamation superimposed upon the flaming numbers '1916'. Above this image a phoenix rises out of the flames, so that the whole links the Rising with the rebirth of the Provisionals in 1969. There has also been a vogue for murals and statues of Cuchulainn, modelled on Oliver Sheppard's statue which stands in the GPO. Yet contemporary republican representations of the mythic Irish hero may have more to do with vying with Protestant iconography than harking back to the GPO. Republican representations take the archetypical symbol of Cuchulainn and refigure him as a heroic warrior assuming the mantle of martyrdom in response to British aggression; in recent years Loyalists have begun to reclaim Ulster mythology as their own, and represent Cuchulainn rather as the defender of Ulster against the Irish. As a character in Frank McGuinness's 1986 play about Ulstermen at the Somme puts it: 'Fenians claim Cuchulainn as their ancestor, but he is ours, for they lay down for centuries and wept in their sorrow, but we took up arms and fought against an ocean.' Two of these rival political murals quite literally mirror one another, since the Republican mural has Cuchulainn facing the 'wrong' way.

At the end of the 1980s, when the trauma of the hunger strikes had begun to recede, and after the Anglo-Irish Agreement, the GPO took centre stage in the Republic again but in a rather different guise: in Neil Jordan's large-budget blockbusting film *Michael Collins*. The film deals with the tumultuous years of the Irish revolution, from 1916 to 1922, tracing Collins's personal and political journey from the moment of the Rising – the initial scenes focus on the iconic bombardment by shells and the surrender from the burning GPO. The first shots show Liam Neeson firing from the second floor of the building; the semi-ruined GPO forms the backdrop to many of the later scenes in the film. Yet the GPO's shift from the political to the cultural stage was not as complete as might be imagined. For the most part enjoyed in the United States as a tragic love story set against the drama of revolution, the film was weighted with historical significance in Ireland. The Irish film censor gave it a certificate for general release, despite the levels of violence, arguing it was important for parents to take their children to see it. Yet the film was criticised for historical inaccuracies and even accused of 'clouding the Peace Process'. Critics argued that in adulating a man who might be seen as the Gerry Adams or Martin McGuinness of his time, the film glorified IRA violence, though the plot was also read as an argument for decommissioning, and the necessity to turn from violence to negotiation and compromise.

The film set for *Michael Collins* was the latest in a series of fake GPOs – the mock-up that was burned at the Military Tatoo in 1935, the burning facades in the Phoenix Park pageants, the plasterboard GPO constructed for the 1966 commemorations in Cork. It was the latest and by far the grandest. Built on the shell of the disused psychiatric

24. *Loyalist mural based on Oliver Sheppard's statue* The Death of Cuchulainn *in Highfield Drive, Belfast. The mural features Cuchulainn as 'Ancient defender of Ulster from Gael attacks', surrounded by the Union Jack, UDA and UFF crests, and a paramilitary guard of honour. The towers in the image are the Irish Tower at Messines in Belgium, and the Ulster Tower at Thiepval in France, both First World War memorials.*

hospital in Grangegorman (where the diarist Thomas King Moylan worked during Easter week) the GPO set was thronged by Dubliners wanting to act as extras in the crowd scenes. On the first day more than 10,000 hopefuls turned up in response to an advertisement, an 'almost uncontrollable

25. *Republican mural based on the Sheppard statue in Falcarragh Road, Lenadoon, Belfast. The mural features Cuchulainn facing towards the left, surrounded by the shields of the four provinces, and names of local volunteers. The caption reads 'Leana an Duin – Unbowed – Unbroken. Saoirse [Freedom]'.*

crowd'. During the weeks of shooting, the film took over Dublin, with streets closed off, traffic rerouted, and in the papers reams of news stories and articles such as 'I was an extra with Michael Collins'.

The street pageant dreamed of by Denis Johnston in 1932

had finally come to pass, though of course not on the actual street. The locals who worked as extras were getting involved in a re-enactment of the events, rather than simply watching a spectacle. Many more visited the set after the filming to walk the streets where history had been made. Except of course it hadn't been made there. One of the oddest aspects of the *Michael Collins* mania was the repeated praise of the set for its accuracy – for the attention to tiny details like the precise brand of discarded cigarette packet. The praise for accuracy was odd since it completely ignored the fact that the area round the GPO itself had been entirely refashioned for the film – instead of the Imperial Hotel opposite the GPO, there was open space; the GPO commanded a view of a wide crossroads. This enabled the cameramen to show the panorama of the building from a distance, to place the British guns directly in front of the building, and for the men to surrender in front of that famous portico. But it certainly wasn't accurate.

During the filming of *Insurrection* in 1966 the actors had apparently been bothered by bystanders interfering in the action, arguing that it didn't happen like that. With *Michael Collins* the citizens of Dublin were involved, but ironically in an entirely fictitious version of events. What Neil Jordan called 'documentary reality' in fact meant creating a balance between mythic or romantic and realistic versions of the event. 'The thing is to make the whole thing real, to take it out of the realm of hagiography and mythology, to make the period come alive as if it was today.' The embarrassing clash between Jordan's avowed intention and the demands of popular movie-making raises questions: can any celebrated revolutionary event conserve its political weight and historical depth indefinitely? As social and cultural contexts shift, as old ideals and ideologies become more remote, is anything left other than pastiche, sentimentality or political romance, of the kind mobilised by Irish republicanism? Right from the beginning, the documentary impulse to record every detail of the Rising had co-existed with the myth-making, rather than contesting or undermining it. As time erodes our grip on the past, political memory, it seems, cannot help but fade into the nostalgic longing to be in a place – or replica of a place – where, in some ever more elusive sense, history was made.

Conclusion

THE FRONT ROOM OF THE NATION

In 1966 the Irish government, keen to involve young people in the commemorations, offered a prize for the best essay imagining the future for the GPO. What would the legacy of the Rising be in 2016? How many could have predicted not only the influence of the Northern crisis but – far harder – the effects of the Celtic Tiger, European integration and the Peace Process on ideas of Irish national identity? The GPO has had to absorb and reflect political, cultural and economic shifts, as well as keep pace with Irish aspirations. It would have been a perceptive schoolchild who could have guessed that, through a combination of street scaping and clever lighting, by the turn of the century the GPO would have begun to look more and more like the White House.

The not-so-subtle Americanisation of the building has been part and parcel of the Irish government's concerted efforts to reclaim the symbolism of 1916 from Sinn Féin and other republican groups. In the run up to the ninetieth anniversary, Fianna Fáil became involved in a huge media push to recover the GPO for the state. Government spokesman Senator Martin Mansergh put it remarkably bluntly:

The real fruit of 1916 was the Irish state, since 1949 a republic. The majority of the different streams involved came to participate in Irish democratic life. Only a small fundamentalist republican fringe refused recognition. Despite appearances, 1916 was not about imposing Dublin rule on a national minority concentrated in northeast Ulster, but was in reality more about going separate ways.

The Irish government – which announced last month that the Irish army would resume its discontinued Easter military parade past the focal point of the rising, and which is setting up a committee to prepare for the 100th anniversary – is determined to disentangle an honourable event from a much later bloody conflict in a divided community that never acquired democratic legitimacy, nor had the support of the Irish state. A parade will not only be about honouring patriots executed by the British, but about celebrating the achievements of modern Ireland.

Apart from the bold rhetorical move of characterising those who did not accept the legitimacy of the Irish state as 'a small fundamentalist republican fringe' (after all, the founder of Fianna Fáil himself, de Valera, refused to accept it for some years), this statement was notable for the surprising suggestion that a kind of mutually agreed partition was part of the goal of 1916: the two parts of the island happily going their separate ways. The point of both claims was to downplay any association of the Irish state with violence and coercion. In 1941 the GPO had symbolised independence and sovereignty, in 1966 it was modernity and by 2006 it was universal democracy.

Government spokesmen tirelessly reiterated the link between the Rising and the state's democratic institutions, pointing out that 1916 was the touchstone for a broad range of constitutional parties. Along with democracy went diversity – MPs and other members of the Northern Assembly were invited to join the celebrations (though Ulster Unionists declined). And along with diversity went a commitment to a kind of commemorative ecumenism. The importance of getting the right balance – the word 'symmetry' was even used – between remembering those who had died in the trenches and those who had died in Dublin had been acknowledged for some time. The restoration of the long-neglected Lutyens First World War Memorial at Islandbridge, and the inauguration of the Island of Ireland Peace Park at Messines in Belgium, where soldiers from the 37th Ulster and 16th Irish divisions died in 1917, were both self-conscious steps in a 'journey of reconciliation'. In a similar gesture, the Easter 1916 commemorations were linked with a second state ceremony held in July to remember those who had died on the Somme. Official publications linked the two ceremonies; commemorative stamps were issued for both events. The dual ritual was described by the government as a sign of the maturity of the nation.

The 2006 public relations exercise was nothing if not carefully orchestrated. Nonetheless, reinstating the Easter parade precipitated a rerun of the debates in 1935 and 1941 over party ownership of the Rising, perhaps particularly because it was clear that 2006 was merely a forerunner to the mega-event that is in preparation for 2016. The militarism of the parade – ironically only possible because of peace in Northern Ireland – provoked accusations that Fianna Fáil were attempting to hijack the Rising in order to outflank Sinn Féin's recent electoral advances. There were calls for the commemorations to focus instead on other aspects of the

Rising, such as universal suffrage and social justice, rather than on militaristic violence.

This touched on an issue that had not troubled people in 1941, nor indeed in 1966 – the 'post-Troubles' version of the Rising as a whole as sectarian and undemocratic, lacking a mandate from the people, and therefore in danger of rekindling respect for paramilitary violence. Given the extreme care taken by the government to associate the Rising with the institutions of the state, and with the results of the Peace Process, it was hard to see how it could be read as support for paramilitarism. Supporters of the revived commemoration pointed out that it had been the loyalist intention to bring down Home Rule – the formation of the Ulster Volunteers, the Larne gun-running – which had been undemocratic. And they rejected the link with paramilitarism. The Volunteers who took over the Post Office had acted not as terrorists but as soldiers engaged in a fight against imperialism. Their imitators were not the Continuity IRA but anti-colonial movements for independence across the world.

In fact what was striking about 2006 was the way in which the national celebration was so empty of national politics. Peaceful, democratic, diverse, the GPO projected global or 'universal values'. It was remarkable how little attention was paid in the media to the personalities and events associated with the Rising. The aim was less to reacquaint Irish people with their own history than to trumpet the achievements of modern Ireland.

In a series of rhetorical gestures the GPO was claimed as central to contemporary politics, the foundation of the current state, but in the same moment depoliticised, or at any rate dehistoricised. With reference to the 2006 parade, a Fine Gael spokesman was quoted as saying, 'We're broadly supportive: the main parties trace their roots back to the GPO. But the current generation have moved so far past this we don't think about it any more. Being Irish is about being successful in music, business and sport. We have so many other role models now.' Getting the GPO to reflect Irish excellence in music, business and sport might seem like a tough call. In part it has been done by emphasising the building's civic and commercial associations, rather than those linking it to the past. The millennium spire which has replaced Nelson's Pillar has no historical meanings at all; it points towards the future (or at any rate, the sky). The widened pavements of O'Connell Street, the trees and sunken lights, all make the area more twenty-first century. In keeping with the new facade, in 2001 there was an attempt to limit the right to protest outside the GPO – the police argued that demonstrations caused problems for the traffic on O'Connell Street – though this move was abandoned in the face of public objections.

The Office of Public Works in Dublin has recently unveiled plans for a more ambitious overhaul of the building. The intention is to create a large glazed courtyard, able to hold 2,000 people, by demolishing the block between the two existing courtyards at the rear of the building. Beneath the courtyard a vast concourse, 'something like the Louvre', will be home to, among other things, a 1916 museum and, of course, shops. The idea is to retain elements of the working post office, but shift them away from the main entrance, which will open instead on to a 'processional route' from the portico to the courtyard, where events such as presidential inaugurations can take place. As an official of the OPW put it: 'This could become the front room of the nation, within a building that's central to the foundation of the State.'

It's always nice to give the front room a makeover, and the mixture of shopping arcade and open space, glass and steel, will be far more in keeping with Ireland's current identity as a rich and forward-looking European nation than the heavy weight of the old nineteenth-century building could ever hope to be. Ever since the early Easter parades it has been the outside of the building that has iconic status, and that will remain the same. Yet, as the building begins the process of becoming a museum to itself, it is a sign that the aura of the Rising has finally dissipated. It is a far cry from Beckett's 'holy ground', the temple to the spirit of 1916 which brought souvenir hunters looking for scraps of metal or stone in the months after the Rising. It would be hard to imagine the current government using fragments of GPO granite to create an independence monument for the World's Fair, as they did in 1939. Among other things this suggests that Fianna Fáil were quite right to believe they could safely reintroduce the GPO into the iconography of the Republic, without upsetting the political order. The Rising is safely in the past.

What seems altogether odder is that even those for whom the GPO represents the unfinished business of the achieved thirty-two-county Republic have begun to celebrate a kind of sanitised version of the building. Sinn Féin still adheres to the goal of reunification of the island, even while they help to govern part of the United Kingdom as members of the Northern Ireland Assembly. The ninetieth anniversary of the Rising coincided with the twenty-fifth anniversary of the hunger strikes, and leaders of the party held a candlelit vigil outside the GPO, where the public protests had been focused in 1981. They are still happy to use the building as a backdrop for keeping in mind the republican struggle; the values of the Proclamation are regularly invoked as central to Sinn Féin politics. But this rhetoric sits somewhat uncomfortably with, for example, the Sinn Féin 'Rebel Dublin' walking tour, designed for tourists and with its centrepiece the GPO. Or the new look Sinn Féin Christmas cards, which showcase the modern landscaped GPO, complete with subtle lighting effects.

The strange thing about Rising kitsch is that the more tasteful it tries to be, the more tasteless it becomes. A post-card of Pearse wearing a halo seems somehow more palatable than a soft-focus contemporary shot of the GPO, with a Christmas greeting in Irish, because the latter is trying so hard to be acceptable. It is now possible to buy online, from republican sites but also from the many sites devoted to Irishry designed for virtual tourists, a huge variety of Rising items – from CDs of rebel songs, GPO keyrings and arty pictures, to reprints of 'original' 1916 ephemera, the photographs and documents that filled the Easter commemorative issues of journals and magazines year after year. Recently this material has been put in the shade by a new wave of Rising authentica, as the documents themselves, as well as the tricolour flown on the building and other original articles, have been put up for sale at public auction.

It is tempting to suggest that now you can buy and sell the Rising it has become meaningless. But this would be too hasty. For all that a framed photograph of a Volunteer's last letter hanging in an Irish kitchen may look like a simulacrum of Rising experience, emptied of aura, it is not entirely hollow. For a small minority it points towards emotional attachment to the republican ideal. For most Irish people its meaning is probably closer to national pride. That people do take pride in the nation, and want to celebrate it, was borne out by the large numbers who turned out for the Easter parade in 2006. It is also evident, paradoxically, in the fact that the GPO is still the focal point for all manner of political protests by interest groups. Campaigns on Tibet, Iraq and Israel suggest that the GPO is still invested with political life. For all the paraphernalia of parades, the GPO is not a politician's building; it is not (yet) a museum. It is a post office and there is still a sense that it belongs to the people.

The same feelings of ownership have motivated people to get involved in the campaign to save 16 Moore Street. They don't want the house where the final council of war was (possibly) held on the Saturday of Easter week to become a supermarket. Although the project of 1916 has been abandoned, particularly as far as remoulding Ireland into an Irish-speaking and self-sufficient nation is concerned, the events of 1916 gave the citizens of the Republic a sense of dignity and achievement, a self-respect that has been woven into the texture of their political life. One of the most important symbolic associations of the GPO is the simple one of national identity. For most citizens of the Republic, national identity is no longer a problem. Arguably this has less to do with the revolutionary will of the insurgents of 1916 than the political institutions of the nation state, yet the GPO crystallises these achievements.

In all this, faith in violent redemptive revolutionary action is conspicuously absent, a fact which may be related to the overall decline in religious observance (who believes in redemption now anyway?), but which probably has more to do with the success of constitutional politics in bringing about change. Irish literature has always kept pace with the changing meanings of the GPO. Judging by contemporary works, there are still myths to explore and debunk, but the issues no longer turn on the opposition between idealism and realism. Sebastian Barry's novel *A Long Long Way* counterpoints the Rising and the First World War; Roddy Doyle's *A Star Called Henry* insists on putting sex and class at the centre of the state's founding moment; Jamie O'Neill's *At Swim Two Boys* links the Rising with a young boy's homosexual awakening. All three novels focus on poverty and class rather than national ideals – their main characters are drawn to the Irish Citizens Army rather than the Volunteers. Yet if these are versions of a new politics of the GPO, we should note that the building, and the Rising itself, are still central to ideas of Irishness.

And, of course, much more than Irishness. If decolonisation, the retreat of imperial power, is one of the 'grand narratives' of the twentieth century, then the siege of the GPO stands close to the beginning of that story. Our notions of the legitimacy of nationalist struggle, of the acceptability of violence in the pursuit of democratic goals, of the role of heroism and sacrifice in political conflict, and of the dignity of small nations in the face of superior force, have all been decisively influenced by what occurred during Easter week in Dublin. Looking back to that inaugural event, and to its reworkings over the years, we can better understand the grip of icons of revolution on the modern political imagination, and the ways in which these emblems can be fought over, reconfigured and abused, in response to vying interests and demands.

The GPO brings together the symbolic story of independent Ireland with the story of Easter week in all its detail. The battle over those details, the determination to get the story right, has shadowed the larger symbolism of the building ever since 1916. The struggle for accuracy, first by participants and eyewitnesses, and later by writers and historians, attests to the emblematic power of the building. For all the work of historical investigation – the questionnaires, the interviews, the witness statements – certain debates won't go away. Which house on Moore Street should be saved from demolition? Should the commemoration take place on Easter Sunday, Easter Monday or 24 April? Where are the phantom steps from which Pearse was said to have read the Proclamation? No amount of retellings of the story will clear up questions like these, which are an integral part of the hold the story has over us. How many days did it last? What really happened?

FURTHER READING

GENERAL

There has been a steady stream of books and articles on the Easter Rising ever since April 1916. New fictional representations, poetry, memoirs and historical studies have often been published around major commemorative years, and the ninetieth anniversary in 2006 was no exception. Charles Townshend's *Easter 1916: The Irish Rebellion* (London, 2005) offers a very well-researched narrative and analysis of the events as a whole, balancing Crown and rebel perspectives, and offering a judicious treatment of the political background to the Rising. Townshend's history has the advantage of access to the hundreds of statements gathered from participants by the Bureau of Military History between 1947 and 1957. These statements were intended to form the basis for a 'history of the movement for Independence', but this was never written, and the statements themselves remained closed to researchers until 2003. Access to this new source of memoir and recollection has been the catalyst for a slew of popular publications about the Rising, such as Annie Ryan (ed.), *Witnesses: Inside the Easter Rising* (Dublin, 2005). Commemoration publications such as Shane Hegarty and Fintan O'Toole (eds), *The Irish Times Book of the 1916 Rising* (Dublin, 2006), draw on the witness statements, bringing together photographs and maps with day-by-day accounts of the events. Gabriel Doherty and Dermot Keogh (eds), *1916: The Long Revolution* (Cork, 2007) reprints the speech given by Mary McAleese which I quote in the Introduction, '1916 – A View from 2006', and also includes new perspectives on public opinion of the Rising, and international perspectives in Europe and the United States. Keith Jeffrey (ed.), *The GPO and the Easter Rising* (Dublin, 2006) reprints participant witness accounts by Father Flanagan and Dick Humphreys (whose account of the week inside the GPO was written initially on toilet paper inside Wakefield Prison) but sets them alongside accounts by the Secretary of the Post Office, Hamilton Norway, his wife and other Post Office officials and civil servants, all of which I draw on in Chapter 1. Jeffrey also reprints St John Ervine's 'The Story of an Irish Rebellion', first published in *Century Magazine* in 1917.

The most vivid popular narrative of the events is still to be found in Max Caulfield, *The Easter Rebellion* (London, 1965). Caulfield augmented the available histories with more than 150 interviews with insurgents and members of the Crown forces. Other useful narratives of the Rising as a whole are Michael Foy and Brian Barton, *The Easter Rising* (Stroud, 1999) and Tim Pat Coogan, *1916: The Easter Rising* (London, 2001). Tim Coates (ed.), *The Irish Uprising 1914–21* (London, 2000) helpfully reprints the 'Report of the Royal Commission on the Rebellion in Ireland, 1916', and the Report of the Royal Commission on the arrest and shooting of Sheehy Skeffington, Dickson and McIntyre, along with other official documents from the period. The political background and implications of the Rising are deftly handled in Chapter 1 of J. J. Lee, *Ireland 1912–1985: Politics and Society* (Cambridge, 1989) and in Michael Laffan, *The Resurrection of Ireland: The*

Sinn Fein Party 1916–1923 (Cambridge, 1999). Joost Auguste-
ijn (ed.), *The Irish Revolution, 1913–1923* (London, 2002) con-
tains an excellent series of essays on the historiography,
definition and impact of the Rising as a whole. See also
Matthew Kelly, *The Fenian Ideal and Irish Nationalism, 1882–
1916* (Woodbridge, 2006).

V. I. Lenin's take on the Rising is published in Owen
Dudley Edwards and Fergus Pyle (eds), *1916: The Easter
Rising* (London, 1968), pp.191–5. For the impact of the Rising
on African-American nationalism, see the introduction
to Robert Hill (ed.) *The Marcus Garvey and Universal Negro
Improvement Association Papers*, Vo1.1 (California, 1983); for
the Chittagong Uprising, see Manini Chatterjee, *Do and Die:
The Chittagong Uprising, 1930–34* (New Delhi and London,
1999).

For the politics and literature of the cultural revival in
Ireland I have drawn on: Declan Kiberd, *Inventing Ireland:
The Literature of the Modern Nation* (London, 1996), especially
the section on 'Revolution and War'; Ben Levitas, *The Theatre
of Nation: Irish Drama and Cultural Nationalism 1890–1916*
(Oxford, 2002); P. J. Mathews, *Revival: The Abbey Theatre,
Sinn Fein, the Gaelic League and the Co-operative Movement*
(Cork, 2003); Mary Trotter, *Ireland's National Theaters* (Syra-
cuse, 2001); and Elaine Sisson, *Pearse's Patriots: St Enda's and
the Cult of Boyhood* (Cambridge, 2004). Of the biographical
studies of Pearse, Ruth Dudley Edwards, *Patrick Pearse, The
Triumph of Failure* (London, 1977) and Seán Farrell Moran,
*Patrick Pearse and the Politics of Redemption: The Mind of the
Easter Rising, 1916* (Washington, 1994) are the most useful.
See also J. J. Lee's article 'In Search of Patrick Pearse', in
Revising the Rising, ed. Máirín Ní Dhonnchadha and Theo
Dorgan (Derry, 1991).

For a perspective on how the cultural politics of the Rising played out in later generations, see in particular James Moran, *Staging the Easter Rising: 1916 as Theatre* (Cork, 2005); William Irwin Thompson, *The Imagination of an Insurrection: Dublin, Easter 1916* (New York, 1967); and Jonathan Githens, *Cultural and Political Nationalism in Ireland: Myths and Memories of the Easter Rising, 1916* (London, 2005).

For reflections on the relationship between history and memory I have drawn on: Pierre Nora, *Realms of Memory: The Construction of the French Past*, 3 vols., trans. Arthur Goldhammer, ed. Lawrence D. Kritzman (New York, 1998); Jay Winter, *Sites of Memory, Sites of Mourning: The Great War in European Cultural History* (Cambridge, 1995); Jay Winter and Emmanuel Sivan (eds), *War and Remembrance in the Twentieth Century* (Cambridge, 1999); David Brett, *The Construction of Heritage* (Cork, 1996); Anthony D. Smith, *The Antiquity of Nations* (Oxford, 2004). For specifically Irish engagement with these debates, see L. M. Geary, *Rebellion and Remembrance in Modern Ireland* (Dublin, 2001); Ian McBride, 'Introduction: Memory and National Identity in Modern Ireland', David Fitzpatrick, 'Commemoration in the Irish Free State: A Chronicle of Embarrassment' and Edna Longley, 'Northern Ireland: Commemoration, Elegy, Forgetting', all in McBride (ed.), *History and Memory in Modern Ireland* (Cambridge, 2001); Ann Dolan, *Commemorating the Irish Civil War, 1923–2000* (Cambridge, 2003); and Jane Leonard, 'Lest We Forget: Irish War Memorials', in David Fitzpatrick (ed.), *Ireland and the First World War* (Dublin, 1986).

1 OCCUPATION, AND 2 DESTRUCTION

On the Post Office in Ireland, see Mairead Reynolds, *A*

History of the Irish Post Office (Dublin, 1983); Ben Novick, 'Postal Censorship in Ireland, 1914–1916', *Irish Historical Studies* 31.123 (1999): 343–56. For the architecture of the new building, see *Irish Builder and Engineer*, 25 March 1916, 8 April 1916. The issue of 13 May 1916 describes the destruction of the building.

Máire Nic Suibhlaigh's recollection of Easter Monday is taken from her memoir (as told to Edward Kenny), *The Splendid Years* (Dublin, 1955). The questionnaires and witness statements collected by Diarmuid Lynch in his investigation of the GPO garrison during the 1930s were used to compile Lynch's study, *The IRB and the 1916 Insurrection* (Cork, 1957). The statements themselves are held in the National Library, MS 15017, and they provide a fascinating 'early' version of the Bureau of Military History statements. I quote here from questionnaires and statements by Michael Boland, Fergus O'Kelly, Austin Kennan, Martin Lynch, Charlie Turner, Michael Knightly and Luke Kennedy. Joseph Cripps's statement is very full, including a great deal of detailed information on medical and chemical supplies, and movement in and out of the building; the story of being turned back from Jervis Street Hospital was recounted by J. J. Doyle; and Frank Henderson provided the information on firing over people's heads to stop them taking bales from barricades, and the daily supply of milk.

Oscar Traynor also provided a very full statement, and his recollection of the 'wipe-out' speech is taken from the Lynch papers, though the story of the shrapnel souvenirs comes from his Bureau of Military History Witness Statement 340; Min Ryan's recollection of Thomas Clarke and the wipe-out appears in a 1966 BBC broadcast, 'Old Ireland Free: The Story of the Easter Rising in 1916' (British Library Sound

Archive NP995); Domhnall Ó Buachalla's wipe-out recollection is reprinted in Annie Ryan (ed.), *Witnesses* (*op. cit.*) and Desmond FitzGerald's is from *Desmond's Rising Memoirs 1913 to Easter 1916* (1968; Dublin, 2006). Desmond Ryan's personal 'wipe-out' conversation with Pearse is taken from *Remembering Sion* (London, 1934), though it also appears in *The Rising: The Complete Story of Easter Week* (Dublin, 1949). For a taste of politically inspired dispute over the 'facts' of Easter week, see Diarmuid Lynch's comments on Ryan's *The Rising*, where he accuses him of idolising Pearse, and of socialist bias causing him to overplay Connolly's role in the events, Chapter 7, *The IRB and the 1916 Insurrection* (*op. cit.*).

I am indebted to Eve Morrison for her advice on Bureau of Military History Witness Statements with particular reference to the GPO. I quote here from Patrick Colgan WS 850; Sean T. O'Kelly WS 1765; Mrs Mulcahy (Min Ryan) WS 399; Eamon Bulfin WS 497; Louise Gavan Duffy WS 216; Tom Byrne WS 564; Francis Daly WS 278 (on making bombs and grenades at Clontarf); Nancy Wyse Power WS 541; Christopher Joseph Brady WS 705; Frank de Burca WS 694; Mary McLoughlin WS 934; Sean McLoughlin WS 209 (on the panic in Moore Lane); Mrs Tom Barry (Lesley Price) WS 1754 (on eating at the officers' table and the story of fetching the priest on Thursday); Ignatius Callender WS 923; and Peadar Bracken WS 361 (on the arrival at the GPO and the instruction to 'man the barricades'). See also Eve Morrison, 'The Bureau of Military History and Female Republican Activism, 1913–23', in Maryann Gialanella Valiulis (ed.), *Gender and Power in Irish History* (Dublin, 2009); Diarmuid Ferriter, '"In Such Deadly Earnest": The Bureau of Military History', *Dublin Review* 6 (Winter 2001–2): 5–15.

The National Library of Ireland holds many original

documents relating to the Rising, and to the GPO. Of particular relevance are Pearse's handwritten copy for the War Bulletins, surrender notes, military orders by General Lowe, passes, Pearse's request for a priest to attend the GPO, the notes to relatives given by insurgents to Father Flanagan, Connolly's orders typewritten by Winifred Carney, memos from British officers to their superiors, Lord Lieutenant announcements from the Vice-Regal lodge, announcements on the Progress of Military Operations against the rebels, photographs of surrenders, Joseph Plunkett's Army Field Book and copies of orders for Easter Manoeuvres. Many of these documents appeared over the years in anniversary issues of magazines and journals such as *An t'Óglac* (April 1926), *The Capuchin Annual* (1936), (1942), (1966) and the *Catholic Bulletin* throughout 1916 and 1917. See also Sean T. O'Kelly, 'Account of Easter Week and After', NLI 27697.

I have also drawn on published recollections by insurgents including James Ryan, 'Inside the GPO', in F. X. Martin (ed.), *The Easter Rising 1916 and University College, Dublin* (Dublin, 1966); Sean MacEntee, *Episode at Easter* (Dublin, 1966); Desmond FitzGerald, *Desmond's Rising* (*op. cit.*); Desmond Ryan, *The Rising: The Complete Story of Easter Week* (Dublin, 1949) and *Remembering Sion* (*op. cit.*); W. J. Brennan-Whitmore, *Dublin Burning: The Easter Rising from Behind the Barricades* (Dublin, 1996); Brian O'Higgins, *The Soldier's Story of Easter Week* (Dublin, 1917); and Kenneth Griffith and Timothy O'Grady, *Curious Journey: An Oral History of Ireland's Unfinished Revolution* (London, 1982). Richard Mulcahy's comment that the rebels had 'no opportunity of effective and soldierly action' appears in a BBC broadcast from 1966, 'Easter Rising 1916', produced by R. D. Smith (British Library Sound Archive T117W).

For the perspective of the onlookers I have drawn on James Stephens, *The Insurrection in Dublin* (Dublin, 1916; Gerrards Cross, 1992); Mrs Hamilton Norway, *The Sinn Fein Rebellion as I Saw It* (London, 1916), later published in Keith Jeffrey (ed.), *The Sinn Fein Rebellion as They Saw it: Mary Louisa and Arthur Hamilton Norway* (Dublin, 1999) and Jeffrey (ed.), *The GPO and the Easter Rising* (*op. cit.*); S. and A. Warwick-Haller (eds), *Letters from Dublin, Easter 1916: The Diary of Alfred Fannin* (Dublin, 1995); Katherine Tynan, *The Years of the Shadow* (London, 1919); and *The Sinn Fein Rebellion Handbook, Easter 1916*, compiled by the *Weekly Irish Times* (Dublin, 1917). I also quote here from Joseph Holloway's diary, NLI MS 1809–1950 and the diary of Thomas King Moylan, NLI MS 9620. In addition to the memoir by St John Ervine published in *Century Magazine*, see also his fictional treatment of the Rising in *Changing Winds* (Dublin and London, 1917).

On Sinn Féin propaganda and German invasion fantasies, see Ben Novick, *Conceiving Revolution: Irish Nationalist Propaganda during the First World War* (Dublin, 2001), pp.120–31; and Roger Casement, *Ireland, Germany and the Freedom of the Seas. A Possible Outcome of the War of 1914?* (New York, n.d.).

3 RECONSTRUCTION

On British socialist and pacifist attitudes to the rising see Douglas Goldring, *The Fortune* (London and Dublin, 1917), his anonymously published *Dublin Explorations and Reflections: By an Englishman* (Dublin, 1917) and *The Fight for Freedom: A Play in Four Acts* (London, 1919); and David Granville, 'The British Labour and Socialist Movement and the 1916 Rising', in Ruán O'Donnell (ed.), *The Impact of the 1916 Rising Among the Nations* (Dublin, 2008); see also the essays in that volume by Ann Matthews, 'Vanguard of the Revolution? The Irish Citizen Army, 1916' and Peter Berresford Ellis, '1916: Insurrection or Rebellion? Making Judgements'.

On the Albert Hall meeting and the British Charter of Freedom, see Bertrand Russell, Letter to Ottoline Morrell, 1 April 1917, in Nicholas Griffin (ed.), *The Selected Letters of Bertrand Russell, The Public Years, 1914–1970* (London, 2001), pp.101–2. I quote here from Sir Francis Vane, 'Incidents of the Rebellion', *Woman's Dreadnought*, 26 Aug 1916, and Patricia Lynch, 'Scenes from the Irish Rebellion', *Woman's Dreadnought*, 13 May 1916; see also S. Pankhurst, P. Lynch and M. O'Callaghan, *Rebel Ireland* (London, 1919). On the No Conscription Fellowship, see Keith Robbins, *The Abolition of War: The 'Peace Movement' in Britain, 1914–1919* (Cardiff, 1976). See also Wayne K. Chapman, 'Leonard Woolf and the Rowntree Political Monthlies, 1916–1922: With the Irish Rebellion as a Case in Point', *South Carolina Review* 34 (2001). G. B. Shaw's letter to the *Daily News* on 10 May 1916, protesting against the executions, is republished in David Pierce (ed.), *Irish Writing in the Twentieth Century: A Reader* (Cork, 2000), pp.239–40.

On perceptions of British militarism, see Hanna Sheehy Skeffington, *British Militarism, As I Have Known It* (New York, 1917); and Monk Gibbon, *Inglorious Soldier* (London, 1968). See also Adrian Hardiman, '"Shot in Cold Blood"': Military Law and Irish Perceptions in the Suppression of the 1916 Rebellion', in Doherty and Keogh (eds), *1916: The Long Revolution* (*op. cit*); and Brian Barton, *From Behind a Closed Door: Secret Court Martial Records of the Easter Rising* (Belfast, 2002). On militarism in general, see David Fitzpatrick, 'Militarism in Ireland, 1900–1922', in Thomas Bartlett and Keith Jeffery (eds.), *A Military History of Ireland* (Cambridge, 1996), pp.379–406; Ben Novick, 'The Arming of Ireland: gun-running and the Great War, 1914–1916', in Adrian Gregory and Senia Paseta, *Ireland and the Great War: 'A war to unite us all'?* (Manchester, 2002), pp.94–112. On female activism and responses see Beth McKillen, 'Irish Feminism and National Separatism, 1914–23', *Eire-Ireland* 17.3 (1982): 52–67; 17.4 (1982): 72–90; Margaret Ward, *Unmanageable Revolutionaries: Women and Irish Nationalism* (London, 1983); Ruth Taillon, *The Women of 1916* (Belfast, 1996); Margaret Ward, 'Nationalism, Pacifism, Internationalism: Louie Bennett, Hanna Sheehy Skeffington and the Problems of "Defining Feminism"', in Anthony Bradley and Maryann Gialanella Valiulis, *Gender and Sexuality in Modern Ireland* (Amherst, 1997).

There is excellent material on the response to the Rising in nationalist Ireland in Michael Wheatley, '"Irreconcilable Enemies" or "Flesh and Blood"? The Irish Party and the Easter Rebels, 1914–1916', in Doherty and Keogh (eds), *1916: The Long Revolution* (*op.cit.*) and Thomas Hennessey, *Dividing Ireland: World War I and Partition* (London and New York, 1998). See also the two appendices, 'The Irish Times on the Easter Rising' and 'Press Reaction to the Rising in General' in Owen Dudley Edwards and Fergus Pyle (eds), *1916: The Easter Rising* (London, 1968). This collection also reprints in full John Dillon's speech in the House of Commons on 11 May 1916; see also F. S. L. Lyons, *John Dillon: A Biography* (London, 1968); Maurice Walsh, *The News from Ireland: Foreign Correspondents and the Irish Revolution* (London, 2008); and Brian P. Murphy, *The Catholic Bulletin and Republican Ireland* (London, 2005). I have consulted newspapers and radical journals published in the aftermath of the Rising, including, for England: *The Times, Illustrated London News, The Nation, New Statesman, John Bull* and *New Witness*; and for Ireland: *Irish Times, Irish Independent, Irish*

Opinion, Irish Nation, Irish Catholic, Irish Builder and Engineer and the *Catholic Bulletin*.

On the relationship between the Rising and the First World War, see Keith Jeffrey, *Ireland and the Great War* (Cambridge, 2000); Jeffrey, 'The Great War and Modern Irish Memory', in T. G. Fraser and K. Jeffrey (eds), *Men, Women and War* (Dublin, 1993); and Jeffrey, 'The First World War and the Rising: Mode, Moment and Memory', in Doherty and Keogh (eds), *1916: The Long Revolution* (*op. cit.*). For an analysis of Christian iconography in the Great War, see 'The Cult of the Fallen Soldier', in George L. Mosse, *Fallen Soldiers: Reshaping the Memory of the World Wars* (Oxford, 1990). See also Terence Denman, 'The Catholic Irish Soldier in the First World War: The "Racial Environment" ', *Irish Historical Studies* 27 (108) (1991): 352–65; David Fitzpatrick (ed.), *Ireland and the First World War* (Dublin, 1986); and Myles Dungan, *They Shall Not Grow Old: Irish Soldiers and the Great War* (Dublin, 1997). On the impact of the Rising on serving soldiers, see Jane Leonard, 'The Reaction of Irish Officers in the British Army to the Easter Rising of 1916', in H. Cecil and P. Liddle (eds), *Facing Armageddon: The First World War Experienced* (London, 1996) and Chapter 4 of Timothy Bowman, *The Irish Regiments in the Great War* (Manchester, 2003). For a convincing sympathetic treatment of Redmond and the war, see D. G. Boyce, 'Nationalism, Unionism and the First World War', in Gregory and Paseta (eds), *Ireland and the Great War* (*op. cit.*), pp.190–216. See also the article by Senia Paseta in the same volume, 'Thomas Kettle: "An Irish Soldier in the Army of Europe?"', pp. 8–27. For Ledwidge's story, see Jon Stallworthy, *Anthem for Doomed Youth: Twelve Soldier Poets of the First World War* (London, 2002).

For early historical accounts of the rebellion, see Warre B.

Wells and N. Marlowe, *A History of the Irish Rebellion of 1916* (Dublin, 1916), which argues, for example, that 'The military plans of the rebels were concerted in close association with the agents of Germany. In their perfection, as in all earlier parts of the negotiations, the entourage of the German Embassy at Washington played a conspicuous part' (p. 128) and that the 'impetuous Labour element' forced through the insurrection despite the countermanding order (p. 140); F. A. McKenzie, *The Irish Rebellion: What Happened and Why* (London, 1916); W. Alison Phillips, *The Revolution in Ireland 1906–1923* (London, 1923); L. G. Redmond-Howard, *Six Days of the Irish Republic: A Narrative and Critical Assessment of the Latest Phase of Irish Politics* (Dublin, 1916); A. S. Green, *Loyalty and Disloyalty* (Dublin, 1918); *The Times History and Encyclopaedia of the War*, Part 102, Vol. 8, 1 August 1916, 'On the Irish Rebellion of April, 1916'. Padraic Colum and James Reidy (eds), *The Irish Rebellion of 1916 and Its Martyrs: Erin's Tragic Easter* (New York, 1916) brings together for a United States audience sketches of the political background, and the events of Easter week and its aftermath, with Royal Commission reports, biographical sketches of the main participants and memoirs. On the first anniversary of the Rising see *Irish Opinion*, 14 April 1917, and 'Rebellion Anniversary', *Irish Independent*, 23 April 1917, p. 3. See also P. S. O'Hegarty, *The Victory of Sinn Fein: How it Won it, and How it Used it* (Dublin, 1924).

I quote here from W. B. Yeats's poems 'Easter 1916' and 'Sixteen Dead Men'. See also his *The Dreaming of the Bones* (1919), a masked play in which an insurgent who has escaped from the GPO refuses to forgive the ghosts of adulterous lovers Dermot MacMurrough and Dervogilla, who are traditionally held responsible for the Norman invasion of Ireland. See Roy Foster, *W. B. Yeats, A Life, II: The Arch Poet* (Oxford, 2003); Helen Vendler, *Our Secret Discipline: Yeats and Lyric Form* (Oxford, 2007); Marjorie Perloff, '"Easter 1916": Yeats's First World War Poem', in Tim Kendall (ed.), *The Oxford Handbook of British and Irish War Poetry* (Oxford, 2007); Wayne K. Chapman, 'Joyce and Yeats: Easter 1916 and the Great War', *New Hibernia Review* 10.3 (2006): 137–51; Chapman, 'Yeats's Dislocated Rebellion Poems and the Great War: The Case of the Wild Swans at Coole and Michael Robartes and the Dancer', *Yeats Annual* 16 (Palgrave, 2005), pp. 71–95; see the section on 'Nationalism and Revolution' in Jonathan Allison (ed.), *Yeats's Political Identities: Selected Essays* (Ann Arbor, 1996); Edna Longley, 'Northern Ireland: Commemoration, Elegy, Forgetting', in McBride (ed.), *History and Memory in Modern Ireland* (*op. cit.*).

Literature critical of the Rising should ideally be separated into material written before 1919, and later works in which the Rising is seen through the lens of the War of Independence and the civil war. Early perspectives include Eimar O'Duffy, *The Wasted Island* (London, 1919: revised 1929), which offers a negative portrait of a Pearse-like character (Austin Mallow), who claims to be a prophet, and insists that the Rising is a 'moral success' despite the military failure. George A. Birmingham, *Up The Rebels!* (London, 1919) is a comic account of bloodless Irish insurrection, complete with porticoed building, Sinn Féiners, romantic nationalists and looting poor. The Quaker schoolmaster Arnold Marsh wrote a play in 1917 entitled *Rebels*, which focuses on the GPO but blames the irruption of violence into Irish life on a Unionist conspiracy (orchestrated by a Belfast arms dealer in league with Germany) whose aim is to destroy Home Rule by stoking Protestant fears in Ulster and drawing Sinn Féin towards doomed armed insurrection. In this he succeeds, but his own son is executed as one of the leaders in the GPO. The play is held at Trinity College Dublin, MS 8365. See also Maurice Dalton, *Sable and Gold* (Dublin, 1922), first performed in 1918. For a slightly later, and odder, take on the Rising, see AE, *The Interpreters* (Dublin, 1922), which is set during a futuristic Irish insurrection, when immense imperial aircraft hover over the rebel city. The focus of the novel is on a group of men in prison and awaiting execution, who debate the spiritual and practical aspects of revolution and the 'appropriate' level of violence. On AE, see Chapter 6 of William Irwin Thompson, *The Imagination of an Insurrection, Dublin, Easter 1916: A Study of an Ideological Movement* (New York, 1967); and Nicholas Allen, *George Russell (AE) and the New Ireland 1905–1930* (Dublin, 2002). See also Brinsley MacNamara, *The Clanking of Chains* (Dublin, 1920).

For English literary responses to the Rising during the war, see May Sinclair's 1917 ferociously pro-war novel *The Tree of Heaven*, where two Irish revolutionary characters see the error of their ways and volunteer for the army (both are killed in France). The novel has some similarities with St John Ervine, *Changing Winds*. In HD's autobiographical novel *Asphodel*, written in the early 1920s, an Irish character harbours a captain escaped from Dublin – based on the colourful Boer war veteran Captain Jack White. ('Captain Ned was an Irish rebel and had reacted from the right thing to this extent, the police might call at any moment … a real officer and a gentleman throwing bombs at the English in Ireland, not getting shot, all very complicated, can't shoot him, his father Trent of Ladyburg.')

The priest who noted the surprising number of manuscript poems in circulation in 1916 was Michael Curran.

His testimony to the Bureau of Military History contained extracts from his diary of Easter week, and is reproduced in Doherty and Keogh (eds), *1916: The Long Revolution* (*op. cit.*). I quote here from 'Ode to Algy' published in the *Irish Nation*, 24 June 1916; *Irish Opinion* published numerous poems throughout 1916 alongside political articles, reviews of Pearse and MacDonagh, and literary essays such as 'On Imagery in Irish Literature' by T. F. O'Rahilly, 9 September 1916. Grace Plunkett's poem 'To The Leaders' was published in *Irish Opinion*, 21 October 1916. A representative selection of Rising poems published in the immediate aftermath of the Rising were reprinted in Edna Fitzhenry (ed.), *Nineteen-Sixteen: An Anthology* (Dublin, 1935). See also Dora Sigerson Shorter, *Love of Ireland and Poems of the Irish Rebellion* (Dublin, 1916). *The Collected Works of Padraic H. Pearse: Plays, Stories, Poems* was brought out by Maunsel in 1917, followed by *Political Writings and Speeches* in 1922. *The Poems of J. M. Plunkett*, ed. Geraldine Plunkett, were published by Talbot Press in Ireland and Fisher Unwin in London in 1916. Fisher Unwin also brought out Thomas MacDonagh's study *Literature in Ireland* and *The Poetical Works of Thomas MacDonagh*, edited by James Stephens in 1916. See also C. Desmond Greaves, *The Easter Rising in Song and Ballad* (London, 1980) and Daniel Corkery, 'Resurrection', *Theatre Arts Monthly* 8.4 (1924): 259–72. Given the emphasis on the Irish language in the Gaelic League and in Pearse's own writings, there is remarkably little Irish writing on the Rising. An exception is Pádraic Ó Conaire's *Seach mBuaidh an Eirghe-Amach* ('The Seven Victories of the Uprising') (Dublin, 1918), stories which focus on mothers, wives, lovers of people in the Rising and the impact on those who were on the sidelines.

4 COMMEMORATION

The full text of the debates on the Anglo-Irish Treaty can be found at www.historical-debates.oireachtas.ie, Vol. 3, 14 December 1921–7 January 1922. For F. X. Martin on the aftermath of the revolution, see '1916 – Myth, Fact and Mystery', *Studia Hibernica* 7 (1967): 7–126; on Sean T. O'Kelly, see Kathleen Clarke, ed. Helen Litton, *Revolutionary Woman, Kathleen Clarke 1878–1972, An Autobiography* (Dublin, 1991). For Kevin O'Higgins on the First World War memorial, see *Dáil Debates*, Vol. 19, 29 March 1927. Patrick Abercrombie's prize-winning town plan for Dublin was published as *Dublin of the Future* (Liverpool, 1922).

For the riots which greeted *The Plough and the Stars*, see Robert G. Lowery (ed.), *A Whirlwind in Dublin: The Plough and the Stars Riots* (Westport, 1984). See also Seamus Deane, 'Irish Politics and O'Casey's Theatre', *Threshold* 24 (1973): 5–16; and *Celtic Revivals: Essays in Modern Irish Literature, 1880–1980* (London, 1985); Nicholas Grene, *The Politics of Irish Drama: Plays in Context from Boucicault to Friel* (Cambridge, 1999); Ronan McDonald, *Tragedy and Irish Literature: Synge, O'Casey, Beckett* (Basingstoke, 2002); and Heinz Kosok, *The Theatre of War: The First World War in British and Irish Drama* (Basingstoke, 2007). For a discussion of both O'Casey and Johnston, see Christopher Morash, *A History of the Irish Theatre, 1601–2000* (Cambridge, 2002). For a dramatic treatment of the controversy over the play, see Colm Tóibín, *Beauty in a Broken Place* (Dublin, 2004). Owen Sheehy Skeffington was interviewed for a 1966 BBC programme about the events and the transcript of the interview is held at NLI 15,015.

Other plays about the Rising which I touch on here are the Easter pageants staged at the Gate, held at the National

Library of Ireland, MacLiammoir Papers, MS 41, 256; Denis Johnston, *The Old Lady Says No!* and *The Scythe and the Sunset* in *The Dramatic Works of Denis Johnston*, Vol. 1 (Gerrards Cross, 1977); Paul Vincent Carroll, *The Conspirators*, in *Irish Stories and Plays* (New York, 1958), pp.111–29; Brendan Behan, *An Giall/The Hostage*, trans and ed. Richard Wall (Gerrards Cross, 1987); Robert Farren, *Lost Light: A Poetic Play about 1916*, in Farren (ed.), *Rime, Gentlemen, Please* (London, 1945); and Donagh MacDonagh, *Easter Christening: A Radio Masque*, *Capuchin Annual* (1942). See also W. B. Yeats, *The Death of Cuchulain* in *The Collected Plays of W. B. Yeats*, Vol. 2, eds. D. R. and R. E. Clark (Basingstoke, 2001). For an English socialist and expressionist take on the Rising, see Montagu Slater, *Easter 1916* (London, 1936).

Denis Johnston's recommendation for open-air re-enactments of the Rising was published under the pseudonym E. W. Tocher in *Motley* 1 (1932), and the debate spilled over into issues 2 and 3. For commemorative memorabilia, see *An tÓglac* 10, 17, 24 April 1926; *Capuchin Annual* (1936), (1942), (1966). I quote Frank Gallagher from the 1936 issue. See also his short stories published under the pseudonym David Hogan, *The Challenge of the Sentry* (Dublin, 1928) and *Dark Mountain* (Dublin, 1931). For perspectives on the violence of the rising see Desmond Ryan, *The Invisible Army* (1932) and Liam O'Flaherty, *Insurrection* (London, 1950). There are also a number of family narratives based around the Rising, often using the trope of brothers divided, or a love triangle, to focus the issue of the civil war. See, for example, Mary Manning's comic novel *Mount Venus* (the subject of a lawsuit by Captain Jack White, who did not like the portrayal of him as a sex-mad ageing revolutionary); Rosamund Jacob, *The Troubled House* (Dublin, 1938); and Margaret Barrington, *My*

Cousin Justin (London, 1939), which includes an unflattering portrayal of her former husband Liam O'Flaherty, as revolutionary on the run. This genre of Rising-related political family saga was later continued by Iris Murdoch in *The Red and the Green* (London, 1965) and Walter Macken in *The Scorching Wind* (London, 1964).

On the statue *The Death of Cuchulainn*, see John Turpin, *Oliver Sheppard 1865–1941: Symbolist Sculptor of the Irish Cultural Revival* (Dublin, 2000). For coverage of the 1935 commemoration, see '1916 Ceremony in Dublin GPO', *Irish Independent*, 18 April 1935, p.11; 'At the GPO', *Irish Press*, 22 April 1935, p.1; 'Dublin GPO Ceremony', *Irish Press*, 22 April 1935, p.2; and 'Easter Week Celebration in Dublin: Significance of 1916 Memorial', *Irish Times*, 22 April 1935, p.8. See also Samuel Beckett, *Murphy* (London, 1993).

5 WHAT STALKED THROUGH THE POST OFFICE?

Study of the 1966 commemoration of the Rising has been greatly helped by the recent publication of a collection of essays edited by Mary E. Daly and Margaret O'Callaghan. *1916 in 1966: Commemorating the Easter Rising* (Dublin 2007) includes excellent articles on almost all aspects of the commemorations – political, artistic, youth, pageant and drama, and their effect on history writing. I draw here on Carole Holohan's essay on 1960s youth and on Roisín Higgins' work on the cultural politics of the commemorations in the Republic. On Northern attitudes to 1916 in 1966, and on Paisley's response, see Margaret O'Callaghan, '"From Casement Park to Toomebridge" – The Commemoration of the Easter Rising in Northern Ireland in 1966', and Catherine O'Donnell, 'Pragmatism Versus Unity: The Stormont

Government and the 1966 Easter Commemoration', both in Daly and O'Callaghan (eds), *1916 in 1966* (*op. cit.*); Matt Treacy, 'Rethinking the Republic: The Republican Movement and 1966', in Ruán O'Donnell (ed.), *The Impact of the 1916 Rising* (*op. cit.*); and Rory O'Dwyer, 'The Golden Jubilee of the 1916 Rising', in Doherty and Keogh (eds), *1916: The Long Revolution* (*op. cit.*). See also the essay in this volume by Gabriel Doherty on the 2006 events, 'The Commemoration of the Ninetieth Anniversary of the Easter Rising'.

Much of RTÉ's radio and television coverage of the 1966 commemorations is available online as part of the 'Cuimhneacháin 1916' exhibition, including news items, drama, extracts from *Insurrection*, and coverage of pageants, speeches and other events. See www.rte.ie/laweb/11/11 _to6_main. html. I refer here to documentaries and films touching on the Rising, including *Mise Eire*, dir. George Morrison (Gael Linn, 1959); *Saoirse*, dir. George Morrison (Gael Linn, 1961); *An Tine Bheo*, dir. Louis Marcus (Gael Linn, 1966); *The Rocky Road to Dublin*, dir. Peter Lennon (Victor Herbert Productions, 1968); *Insurrection*, dir. Louis Lentin (RTÉ, 1966); *Michael Collins*, dir. Neil Jordan (Warner Brothers, 1996). See also Harvey O'Brien, *The Real Ireland: The Evolution of Ireland in Documentary Film* (Manchester, 2004); Lance Pettit, *Screening Ireland: Film and Television Representation* (Manchester, 2000); and Neil Jordan, *Michael Collins: Screenplay and Film Diary* (London, 1996).

For Conor Cruise O'Brien's changing view of the Rising, see 'The Embers of Easter 1916–1966', in Edwards and Pyle (eds), *1916: The Easter Rising* (*op. cit.*), and *Ancestral Voices: Religion and Nationalism in Ireland* (Chicago, 1995). See also Garret FitzGerald, 'The Significance of 1916', *Studies* 55 (Spring 1966): 29–37.

For popular fiftieth-anniversary books on the Rising, see for example the Easter Commemoration issue of the *Irish Digest* (Vol. 8, Easter 1966), which includes Lemass's comments about economic consolidation; Department of External Affairs, *Cuimhneachán 1916–1966: A Record of Ireland's Commemoration of the 1916 Rising* (Dublin, 1966); Charles Duff, *Six Days to Shake an Empire* (London, 1966); and Roger McHugh ed., *Dublin 1916: An Illustrated Anthology* (London, 1966).

For scholarly historical work produced around the fiftieth anniversary, see F. X. Martin (ed.), *Leaders and Men of the Easter Rising: Dublin 1916* (London, 1967); Leon Ó Broin, *Dublin Castle and the 1916 Rising* (Dublin, 1966); F. X. Martin, 'Select Documents: Eoin MacNeill on the 1916 Rising', *Irish Historical Studies* 12 (March 1961): 226–71; F. X. Martin, '1916 – Myth, Fact and Mystery', *Studia Hibernica* 7 (1967): 7–126; Martin, 'The 1916 Rising – A Coup d'État or a "Bloody Protest"?', *Studia Hibernica* 8 (1968); and Kevin B. Nowlan (ed.), *The Making of 1916: Studies in the History of the Rising* (Dublin, 1969). See also D. G. Boyce, '1916, Interpreting the Rising', in Boyce and Alan O'Day (eds), *The Making of Modern Irish History: Revisionism and the Revisionist Controversy* (London, 1996), pp.163–87.

Literary responses to the fiftieth anniversary include Eugene McCabe, *Pull Down a Horseman* (Oldcastle, Co. Meath, 1979), which focuses on the meeting between Pearse and Connolly in January 1916 and the debate over nationalism or social revolution. Tom Murphy, *The Patriot Game* (London, 1992) was written for the fiftieth anniversary but not performed until the seventy-fifth. Eoghan Ó Tuarisc, *Dé Luain* (Dublin, 1966) is a rare experimental Irish-language treatment of the Rising. The entire novel is set over the Sunday night and Monday morning of 23 and 24 April 1916.

The style is impressionistic, ending with Pearse's internal monologue as he reads the Proclamation on the 'steps' of the GPO: 'We stand on the steps between the stone columns as if we were on a Greek stage before the King's palace, acting out the tragedy again and again for the crowd.' See also Seamus Heaney, 'Requiem for the Croppies', *Door into the Dark* (London, 1969).

On the history of the Northern republican movement, see Richard English, *Armed Struggle: A History of the IRA* (London, 2003), who quotes Martin McGuinness on the hunger strikes and 1916; and Richard Bourke, *Peace in Ireland: The War of Ideas* (London, 2003). For Jim McVeigh's statement, see 'Interview', *Saoirse* 32, 11 March 2006. See also David Beresford, *Ten Men Dead: The Story of the 1981 Hunger Strike* (London, 1987); the three-volume series by Bill Rolston, *Drawing Support: Murals in the North of Ireland* (Belfast, 1992, 1995, 2003); and Jane Leonard, *Memorials to the Casualties of Conflict: Northern Ireland 1969–1997* (Belfast, 1997). See also Frank McGuinness, *Observe the Sons of Ulster Marching Towards the Somme* (Faber, 1986).

On the Irish government's decision not to commemorate the seventy-fifth anniversary, see *Revising the Rising*, ed. Máirín Ní Dhonnchadha and Theo Dorgan (Derry, 1991), especially the essays by Declan Kiberd, Edna Longley and Seamus Deane; Dermot Bolger (ed.), *16 on 16* (Dublin, 1989); Bobby Ballagh, '1916 – Goodbye to All That?', *Irish Reporter* 2 (1991): 6–8; and Colm Tóibín, 'New Ways of Killing Your Father', *London Review of Books*, 18 November 1993. Recent literary treatments of the Rising include Roddy Doyle, *A Star Called Henry* (London, 1999), much of which is set in the GPO; Sebastian Barry, *A Long Long Way* (London, 2005); and Jamie O'Neill, *At Swim Two Boys* (London, 2001).

On the political geography of contemporary Dublin, see Andrew Kincaid, *Postcolonial Dublin: Imperial Legacies and the Built Environment* (London, 2006); and Judith Hill, *Irish Public Sculpture: A History* (Dublin, 1998). For Dublin rebellion tours, see Mick O'Farrell, *A Walk Through Rebel Dublin 1916* (Cork, 1999) and Conor Kostick and Lorcan Collins, *The Easter Rising: A Guide to Dublin in 1916* (Dublin, 2000).

LIST OF ILLUSTRATIONS

ACKNOWLEDGEMENTS

I am grateful to the following people for reading passages or chapters, discussing points, or tracking down wayward bits of information: Nadia Atia, Michele Barrett, Richard Bourke, Wayne Chapman, Santanu Das, Markman Elllis, Luke Gibbons, Ultán Gillen, Lisa Godson, Peter Howarth, Peter Jameson, Keith Jeffery, Commandant Victor Laing, Joe Lee, Ben Levitas, Maria Luddy, Ian McBride, Deirdre McMahon, Eve Morrison, Brian Ó Conchubhair, Eunan O'Halpin, Geraldine Parsons, Ian Patterson, Keith Robbins, Dan Todman, and Maurice Walsh. The archivists at the Irish Military Archives, the National Archives, the National Library of Ireland and the British Library, including the Sound Archive and the Newspaper Library, have been especially helpful. Mary Beard and Peter Carson both read the complete manuscript and I am extremely grateful to them, and to Penny Daniel at Profile, for the care and attention they gave to it. Seamus Heaney's 'Requiem for the Croppies', from *Door into the Dark* (1969) is reproduced with the kind permission of Faber and Faber and Farrar, Straus and Giroux. Thanks for their patience and advice to Peter Dews, and Jacob, Luan and Philomena Wills, and to Luan for his technical know-how.

INDEX

PROFILES IN HISTORY

The *Profiles in History* series will explore iconic events and relationships in history. Each book will start from the historical moment: what happened? But each will focus too on the fascinating and often surprising afterlife of the story concerned.

Profiles in History is under the general editorship of Mary Beard.